MEN IN WAR

MEN IN WAR

BY ADOLF ANDREAS LATZKO

Short Story Index Reprint Series

BOOKS FOR LIBRARIES PRESS
FREEPORT, NEW YORK

First Published 1918
Reprinted 1970

STANDARD BOOK NUMBER:
8369-3465-2

LIBRARY OF CONGRESS CATALOG CARD NUMBER:
71-116961

PRINTED IN THE UNITED STATES OF AMERICA

DEDICATED TO
FRIEND AND FOE

"I am convinced the time will come when all will think as I do."

CONTENTS

OFF TO WAR

I

OFF TO WAR

THE time was late in the autumn of the
second year of the war; the place, the
garden of a war hospital in a small Austrian
town, which lay at the base of wooded hills,
sequestered as behind a Spanish wall, and still
preserving its sleepy contented outlook upon
existence.

Day and night the locomotives whistled by.
Some of them hauled to the front trains of soldiers singing and hallooing, high-piled bales of
hay, bellowing cattle and ammunition in
tightly-closed, sinister-looking cars. The others, in the opposite direction, came creeping
homeward slowly, marked by the bleeding
cross that the war has thrown upon all walls
and the people behind them. But the great
madness raced through the town like a hurri-

cane, without disturbing its calm, as though
the low, brightly colored houses with the old-
fashioned ornate façades had tacitly come to
the sensible agreement to ignore with aristocratic reserve this arrogant, blustering fellow,
War, who turned everything topsy-turvy.

In the parks the children played unmo-
lested with the large russet leaves of the old
chestnut trees. Women stood gossiping in
front of the shops, and somewhere in every
street a girl with a bright kerchief on her head
could be seen washing windows. In spite of
the hospital flags waving from almost every
house, in spite of innumerable bulletin boards,
notices and sign-posts that the intruder had
thrust upon the defenseless town, peace still
seemed to prevail here, scarcely fifty miles
away from the butchery, which on clear nights
threw its glow on the horizon like an artificial
illumination. When, for a few moments at a
time, there was a lull in the stream of heavy,
snorting automobile trucks and rattling drays,
and no train happened to be rumbling over the

railroad bridge and no signal of trumpet or
clanking of sabres sounded the strains of war,
then the obstinate little place instantly showed
up its dull but good-natured provincial face,
only to hide it again in resignation behind its
ill-fitting soldier's mask, when the next automobile from the general staff came dashing
around the corner with a great show of importance.

To be sure the cannons growled in the distance, as if a gigantic dog were crouching way
below the ground ready to jump up at the
heavens, snarling and snapping. The muffled barking of the big mortars came from over
there like a bad fit of coughing from a sick-
room, frightening the watchers who sit with
eyes red with crying, listening for every sound
from the dying man. Even the long, low rows
of houses shrank together with a rattle and
listened horrorstruck each time the coughing
convulsed the earth, as though the stress of
war lay on the world's chest like a nightmare.

The streets exchanged astonished glances,

blinking sleepily in the reflection of the night-lamps that inside cast their merrily dancing shadows over close rows of beds. The rooms, choke-full of misery, sent piercing shrieks and wails and groans out into the night. Every human sound coming through the windows fell upon the silence like a furious attack. It was a wild denunciation of the war that out there at the front was doing its work, discharging mangled human bodies like so much offal and filling all the houses with its bloody refuse.

But the beautiful wrought-iron fountains continued to gurgle and murmur compla-cently, prattling with soothing insistence of the days of their youth, when men still had the time and the care for noble lines and curves, and war was the affair of princes and adven-turers. Legend popped out of every corner and every gargoyle, and ran on padded soles through all the narrow little streets, like an invisible gossip whispering of peace and com-fort. And the ancient chestnut trees nodded assent, and with the shadows of their out-

spread fingers stroked the frightened façades
to calm them. The past grew so lavishly out
of the fissured walls that any one coming within
their embrace heard the plashing of the fountains above the thunder of the artillery; and
the sick and wounded men felt soothed and
listened from their fevered couches to the talkative night outside. Pale men, who had been
carried through the town on swinging stretch-
ers, forgot the hell they had come from; and
even the heavily laden victims tramping
through the place on a forced march by night
became softened for a space, as if they had
encountered Peace and their own unarmed
selves in the shadow of the columns and the
flower-filled bay-windows.

The same thing took place with the war in
this town as with the stream that came down
from out of the mountains in the north, foaming with rage at each pebble it rolled over. At
the other end of the town, on passing the last
houses, it took a tender leave, quite tamed and
subdued, murmuring very gently, as if tread-

ing on tiptoe, as if drowsy with all the dreaminess it had reflected. Between wide banks, it stepped out into the broad meadowland, and circled about the war hospital, making almost an island of the ground it stood on. Thick-stemmed sycamores cast their shadow on the hospital, and from three sides came the murmur of the slothful stream mingled with the rustling of the leaves, as if the garden, when twilight fell, was moved by compassion and sang a slumber song for the lacerated men, who had to suffer in rank and file, regimented up to their very death, up to the grave, into which they—unfortunate cobblers, tinkers, peasants, and clerks—were shoved to the accompaniment of salvos from big-mouthed cannon.

The sound of taps had just died away, and the watchmen were making their rounds, when they discovered three men in the deep shadow of the broad avenue, and drove them into the house.

"Are you officers, eh?" the head-watchman,

a stocky corporal of the landsturm, with grey on his temples, growled and blustered good-naturedly. "Privates must be in bed by nine o'clock." To preserve a show of authority he added with poorly simulated bearishness: "Well, are you going or not?"

He was about to give his usual order, "Quick, take to your legs!" but caught himself just in time, and made a face as though he had swallowed something.

The three men now hobbling toward the entrance for inmates, would have been only too glad to carry out such an order. However, they had only two legs and six clattering crutches between them. It was like a living picture posed by a stage manager who has an eye for symmetry. On the right went the one whose right leg had been saved, on the left went his counterpart, hopping on his left leg, and in the middle the miserable left-over of a human body swung between two high crutches, his empty trousers raised and pinned across his chest, so that the whole man could have gone comfortably into a cradle.

The corporal followed the group with his eyes, his head bent and his fists clenched, as if bowed down beneath the burden of the sight. He muttered a not exactly patriotic oath and spat out a long curve of saliva with a hiss from between his front teeth. As he was about to turn and go on his round again, a burst of laughter came from the direction of the officers' wing. He stood still and drew in his head as if from a blow on the back of his neck, and a gleam of ungovernable hatred flitted over his broad, good-natured peasant face. He spat out again, to soothe his feelings, then took a fresh start and passed the merry company with a stiff salute.

The gentlemen returned the salute carelessly. Infected by the coziness that hung over the whole of the town like a light cloud, they were sitting chatting in front of the hospital on benches moved together to form a square. They spoke of the war and—laughed,

laughed like happy schoolboys discussing the miseries of examinations just gone through. Each had done his duty, each had had his ordeal, and now, under the protection of his wound, each sat there in the comfortable expectation of returning home, of seeing his people again, of being fêted, and for at least two whole weeks, of living the life of a man who is not tagged with a number.

The loudest of the laughers was the young lieutenant whom they had nicknamed the Mussulman because of the Turkish turban he wore as officer of a regiment of Bosnians. A shell had broken his leg, and done its work thoroughly. For weeks already the shattered limb had been tightly encased in a plaster cast, and its owner, who went about on crutches, cherished it carefully, as though it were some precious object that had been confided to his care.

On the bench opposite the Mussulman sat two gentlemen, a cavalry officer, the only one on the active list, and an artillery officer, who

in civil life was a professor of philosophy, and
so was called "Philosopher" for short. The
cavalry captain had received a cut across his
right arm, and the Philosopher's upper lip had
been ripped by a splinter from a grenade.
Two ladies were sitting on the bench that
leaned against the wall of the hospital, and
these three men were monopolizing the conversation with them, because the fourth man
sat on his bench without speaking. He was
lost in his own thoughts, his limbs twitched,
and his eyes wandered unsteadily. In the war
he was a lieutenant of the landsturm, in civil
life a well-known composer. He had been
brought to the hospital a week before, suffering from severe shock. Horror still gloomed
in his eyes, and he kept gazing ahead of him
darkly. He always allowed the attendants at
the hospital to do whatever they wanted to
him without resistance, and he went to bed or
sat in the garden, separated from the others
as by an invisible wall, at which he stared and
stared. Even the unexpected arrival of his

pretty, fair wife had not resulted in dispelling for so much as a second the vision of the awful occurrence that had unbalanced his mind. With his chin on his chest he sat without a smile, while she murmured words of endearment; and whenever she tried to touch his poor twitching hands with the tips of her fingers, full of infinite love, he would jerk away as if seized by a convulsion, or under torture.

Tears rolled down the little woman's cheeks —cheeks hungry for caresses. She had fought her way bravely through the zones barred to civilians until she finally succeeded in reaching this hospital in the war zone. And now, after the great relief and joy of finding her husband alive and unmutilated, she suddenly sensed an enigmatic resistance, an unexpected obstacle, which she could not beg away or cry away, as she had used to do. There was a something there that separated her mercilessly from the man she had so yearned to see.

She sat beside him impatiently, tortured by

her powerlessness to find an explanation for
the hostility that he shed around him. Her
eyes pierced the darkness, and her hands always went the same way, groping forward
timidly, then quickly withdrawing as though
scorched when his shrinking away in hatred
threw her into despair again.

It was hard to have to choke down her grief
like this, and not burst out in reproach and
tear this secret from her husband, which he in
his misery still interposed so stubbornly between himself and his one support. And it
was hard to simulate happiness and take part
in the airy conversation; hard always to have
to force some sort of a reply, and hard not to
lose patience with the other woman's perpet-
ual giggling. It was easy enough for *her*.
She knew that her husband, a major-general,
was safe behind the lines on the staff of a high
command. She had fled from the ennui of a
childless home to enter into the eventful life of
the war hospital.

The major's wife had been sitting in the

garden with the gentlemen ever since seven o'clock, always on the point of leaving, quite ready to go in her hat and jacket, but she let herself be induced again and again to remain a little longer. She kept up her flirtatious conversation in the gayest of spirits, as if she had no knowledge of all the torments she had seen during the day in the very house against which she was leaning her back. The sad little woman breathed a sigh of relief when it grew so dark that she could move away from the frivolous chatterbox unnoticed.

And yet in spite of her titillating conversation and the air of importance with which she spoke of her duties as a nurse, the Frau Major was penetrated by a feeling that, without her being conscious of it, raised her high above herself. The great wave of motherliness that had swept over all the women when the fatal hour struck for the men, had borne her aloft, too. She had seen the three men with whom she was now genially exchanging light nothings come to the hospital—like thousands of others—streaming with blood, helpless, whimpering with pain. And something of the joy of the hen whose brood has safely hatched warmed her coquetry.

Since the men have been going for months, crouching, creeping on all fours, starving, carrying their own death as mothers carry their children; since suffering and waiting and the passive acceptance of danger and pain have reversed the sexes, the women have felt strong, and even in their sensuality there has been a little glimmer of the new passion for mothering.

The melancholy wife, just arrived from a region in which the war exists in conversation only, and engrossed in the one man to the exclusion of the others, suffered from the sexless familiarity that they so freely indulged in there in the shadow of death and agony. But the others were at home in the war. They spoke its language, which in the men was a mixture of obstinate greed for life and a paradoxical softness born of a surfeit of brutality;

while in the woman it was a peculiar, garru-
lous cold-bloodedness. She had heard so
much of blood and dying that her endless curiosity gave the impression of hardness and
hysterical cruelty.

The Mussulman and the cavalry officer were
chaffing the Philosopher and poking fun at
the phrase-mongers, hair-splitters, and other
wasters of time. They took a childish delight in his broad smile of embarrassment at
being teased in the Frau Major's presence,
and she, out of feminine politeness, came to
the Philosopher's rescue, while casting amor-
ous looks at the others who could deal such
pert blows with their tongues.

"Oh, let the poor man alone," she laughed
and cooed. "He's right. War is horrible.
These two gentlemen are just trying to get
your temper up." She twinkled at the
Philosopher to soothe him. His good nature
made him so helpless.

The Philosopher grinned phlegmatically
and said nothing. The Mussulman, setting

his teeth, shifted his leg, which in its white bandage was the only part of him that was visible, and placed it in a more comfortable position on the bench.

"The Philosopher?" he laughed. "As a matter of fact, what does the Philosopher know about war? He's in the artillery. And war is conducted by the infantry. Don't you know that, Mrs. ——?"

"I am not Mrs. here. Here I am Sister Engelberta," she cut in, and for a moment the expression on her face became almost serious.

"I beg your pardon, Sister Engelberta. Artillery and infantry, you see, are like husband and wife. We infantrymen must bring the child into the world when a victory is to be born. The artillery has only the pleasure, just like a man's part in love. It is not until after the child has been baptized that he comes strutting out proudly. Am I not right, Captain?" he asked, appealing to the cavalry officer. "You are an equestrian on foot now, too."

The captain boomed his assent. In his summary view, members of the Reichstag who refused to vote enough money for the military, Socialists, pacifists, all men, in brief, who lectured or wrote or spoke superfluous stuff and lived by their brains belonged in the same category as the Philosopher. They were all "bookworms."

"Yes, indeed," he said in his voice hoarse from shouting commands. "A philosopher like our friend here is just the right person for the artillery. Nothing to do but wait around on the top of a hill and look on. If only they don't shoot up our own men! It is easy enough to dispose of the fellows on the other side, in front of us. But I always have a devilish lot of respect for you assassins in the back. But let's stop talking of the war. Else I'll go off to bed. Here we are at last with two charming ladies, when it's been an age since we've seen a face that isn't covered with stubble, and you still keep talking of that damned shooting. Good Lord, when I was in the hospital train and the first girl came in with a white cap on her curly light hair, I'd have liked to hold her hand and just keep looking and looking at her. Upon my word of honor, Sister Engelberta, after a while the shooting gets to be a nuisance. The lice are worse. But the worst thing of all is the complete absence of the lovely feminine. For five months to see nothing but men—and then all of a sudden to hear a dear clear woman's voice! That's the finest thing of all. It's worth going to war for."

The Mussulman pulled his mobile face flashing with youth into a grimace.

"The finest thing of all! No, sir. To be quite frank, the finest thing of all is to get a bath and a fresh bandage, and be put into a clean white bed, and know that for a few weeks you're going to have a rest. It's a feeling like —well, there's no comparison for it. But, of course, it is very nice, too, to be seeing ladies again."

The Philosopher had tilted his round fleshy

Epicurean head to one side, and a moist sheen came into his small crafty eyes. He glanced at the place where a bright spot in the almost palpable darkness suggested the Frau Major's white dress, and began to tell what he thought, very slowly in a slight sing-song.

"The finest thing of all, I think, is the quiet —when you have been lying up there in the mountains where every shot is echoed back and forth five times, and all of a sudden it turns absolutely quiet—no whistling, no howling, no thundering—nothing but a glorious quiet that you can listen to as to a piece of music! The first few nights I sat up the whole time and kept my ears cocked for the quiet, the way you try to catch a tune at a distance. I believe I even howled a bit, it was so delightful to listen to no sound."

The captain of cavalry sent his cigarette flying through the night like a comet scattering sparks, and brought his hand down with a thump on his knee.

"There, there, Sister Engelberta, did you

get that?" he cried sarcastically. " 'Listen to
no sound.' You see, that's what's called philosophy. I know something better than that,
Mr. Philosopher, namely, not to hear what you
hear, especially when it's such philosophical
rubbish."

They laughed, and the man they were teas-
ing smiled good-naturedly. He, too, was
permeated by the peacefulness that floated into
the garden from the sleeping town. The cavalryman's aggressive jokes glided off without
leaving a sting, as did everything else that
might have lessened the sweetness of the few
days still lying between him and the front.
He wanted to make the most of his time, and
take everything easily with his eyes tight shut,
like a child who has to enter a dark room.

The Frau Major leaned over to the Philosopher.

"So opinions differ as to what was the finest thing," she said; and her breath came more
rapidly. "But, tell me, what was the most
awful thing you went through out there? A lot

of the men say the drumfire is the worst, and a lot of them can't get over the sight of the first man they saw killed. How about you?"

The Philosopher looked tortured. It was a theme that did not fit into his programme. He was casting about for an evasive reply when an unintelligible wheezing exclamation drew all eyes to the corner in which the landsturm officer and his wife were sitting. The others had almost forgotten them in the darkness and exchanged frightened glances when they heard a voice that scarcely one of them knew, and the man with the glazed eyes and uncertain gestures, a marionette with broken joints, began to speak hastily in a falsetto like the crowing of a rooster.

"What was the most awful thing? The only awful thing is the going off. You go off to war—and they let you go. That's the awful thing."

A cold sickening silence fell upon the company. Even the Mussulman's face lost its perpetually happy expression and stiffened in embarrassment. It had come so unexpectedly and sounded so unintelligible. It caught them by the throat and set their pulses bounding—perhaps because of the vibrating of the voice that issued from the twitching body, or because of the rattling that went along with it, and made it sound like a voice broken by long sobbing.

The Frau Major jumped up. She had seen the landsturm officer brought to the hospital strapped fast to the stretcher, because his sobbing wrenched and tore his body so that the bearers could not control him otherwise. Something inexpressibly hideous—so it was said—had half robbed the poor devil of his reason, and the Frau Major suddenly dreaded a fit of insanity. She pinched the cavalryman's arm and exclaimed with a pretense of great haste:

"My goodness! There's the gong of the last car. Quick, quick," addressing the sick man's wife, "quick! We must run."

They all rose. The Frau Major passed her

arm through the unhappy little woman's and
urged with even greater insistence:

"We'll have a whole hour's walk back to
town if we miss the car."

The little wife, completely at a loss, her
whole body quivering, bent over her husband
again to take leave. She was certain that his
outburst had reference to her and held a grim
deadly reproach, which she did not comprehend. She felt her husband draw back and
start convulsively under the touch of her lips.
And she sobbed aloud at the awful prospect of
spending an endless night in the chilly neg-
lected room in the hotel, left alone with this
tormenting doubt. But the Frau Major
drew her along, forcing her to run, and did not
let go her arm until they had passed the sen-
tinel at the gate and were out on the street.
The gentlemen followed them with their eyes,
saw them reappear once again on the street in
the lamplight, and listened to the sound of the
car receding in the distance. The Mussulman picked up his crutches, and winked at the

Philosopher significantly, and said something with a yawn about going to bed. The cavalry officer looked down at the sick man curiously and felt sorry for him. Wanting to give the poor devil a bit of pleasure, he tapped him on his shoulder and said in his free and easy way:

"You've got a chic wife, I must say. I congratulate you."

The next instant he drew back startled. The pitiful heap on the bench jumped up suddenly, as though a force just awakened had tossed him up from his seat.

"Chic wife? Oh, yes. Very dashing!" came sputtering from his twitching lips with a fury that cast out the words like a seething stream. "She didn't shed a single tear when I left on the train. Oh, they were all very dashing when we went off. Poor Dill's wife was, too. Very plucky! She threw roses at him in the train and she'd been his wife for only two months." He chuckled disdainfully and clenched his teeth, fighting hard to suppress the tears burning in his threat. "Roses!

He-he! And 'See you soon again!' They were all so patriotic! Our colonel congratulated Dill because his wife had restrained herself so well—as if he were simply going off to maneuvers."

The lieutenant was now standing up. He swayed on his legs, which he held wide apart, and supported himself on the cavalry captain's arm, and looked up into his face expectantly with unsteady eyes.

"Do you know what happened to him—to Dill? I was there. Do you know what?"

The captain looked at the others in dismay.

"Come on—come on to bed. Don't excite yourself," he stammered in embarrassment.

With a howl of triumph the sick man cut him short and snapped in an unnaturally high voice:

"You don't know what happened to Dill, you don't? We were standing just the way we are now, and he was just going to show me the new photograph that his wife had sent him —his brave wife, he-he, his restrained wife.

Oh yes, restrained! That's what they all were—all prepared for anything. And while we were standing there, he about to show me the picture, a twenty-eighter struck quite a distance away from us, a good two-hundred yards. We didn't even look that way. Then all of a sudden I saw something black come flying through the air—and Dill fell over with his dashing wife's picture in his hand and a boot, a leg, a boot with the leg of a baggage soldier sticking in his head—a soldier that the twenty-eighter had blown to pieces far away from where we stood."

He stopped for an instant and stared at the captain triumphantly. Then he went on with a note of spiteful pride in his voice, though every now and then interrupted by a peculiar gurgling groan.

"Poor Dill never said another word—Dill with the spur sticking in his skull, a regular cavalry spur, as big as a five-crown piece. He only turned up the whites of his eyes a little and looked sadly at his wife's picture, that she should have permitted such a thing as that. Such a thing as that! Such a thing! It took four of us to pull the boot out—four of us. We had to turn it and twist it, until a piece of his brain came along—like roots pulled up— like a jellyfish—a dead one—sticking to the spur."

"Shut up!" the captain yelled furiously, and tore himself away and walked into the house cursing.

The other two looked after him longingly, but they could not let the unfortunate man stay there by himself. When the captain had withdrawn his arm, he had fallen down on the bench again and sat whimpering like a whipped child, with his head leaning on the back. The Philosopher touched his shoulder gently, and was about to speak to him kindly and induce him to go into the house when he started up again and broke out into an ugly, snarling laugh.

"But we tore her out of him, his dashing wife. Four of us had to tug and pull until

she came out. I got him rid of her. Out
with her! She's gone. All of them are gone.
Mine is gone, too. Mine is torn out, too. All
are being torn out. There's no wife any more!
No wife any more, no——"

His head bobbed and fell forward. Tears
slowly rolled down his sad, sad face.

The captain reappeared followed by the little assistant physician, who was on night duty.

"You must go to bed now, Lieutenant," the
physician said with affected severity.

The sick man threw his head up and stared
blankly at the strange face. When the physician repeated the order in a raised voice, his
eyes suddenly gleamed, and he nodded approv-
ingly.

"Must go, of course," he repeated eagerly,
and drew a deep sigh. "We all must go.
The man who doesn't go is a coward, and they
have no use for a coward. That's the very
thing. Don't you understand? Heroes are
the style now. The chic Mrs. Dill wanted a
hero to match her new hat. Ha-ha! That's

why poor Dill had to go and lose his brains.
I, too—you, too—we must go die. You must
let yourself be trampled on—your brains
trampled on, while the women look on—chic
—because it's the style now."

He raised his emaciated body painfully,
holding on to the back of the bench, and eyed
each man in turn, waiting for assent.

"Isn't it sad?" he asked softly. Then his
voice rose suddenly to a shriek again, and the
sound of his fury rang out weirdly in the garden. "Weren't they deceiving us, eh? I'd
like to know—weren't they cheats? Was I an
assassin? Was I a ruffian? Didn't I suit her
when I sat at the piano playing? We were
expected to be gentle and considerate! Considerate! And all at once, because the fashion changed, they had to have murderers. Do
you understand? Murderers!"

He broke away from the physician, and
stood swaying again, and his voice gradually
sank to a complaining sound like the thick
strangulated utterance of a drunkard.

"My wife was in fashion too, you know. Not a tear! I kept waiting and waiting for her to begin to scream and beg me at last to get out of the train, and not go with the others —beg me to be a coward for her sake. Not one of them had the courage to. They just wanted to be in fashion. Mine, too! Mine, too! She waved her handkerchief just like all the rest."

His twitching arms writhed upwards, as though he were calling the heavens to witness.

"You want to know what was the most awful thing?" he groaned, turning to the Philosopher abruptly. "The disillusionment was the most awful thing—the going off. The war wasn't. The war is what it has to be. Did it surprise you to find out that war is horrible? The only surprising thing was the going off. To find out that the women are horrible—that was the surprising thing. That they can smile and throw roses, that they can give up their men, their children, the boys they have put to bed a thousand times and pulled the

covers over a thousand times, and petted and
brought up to be men. That was the surprise! That they gave us up—that they sent
us—*sent* us! Because every one of them
would have been ashamed to stand there without a hero. That was the great disillusionment. Do you think we should have gone if
they had not sent us? Do you think so? Just
ask the stupidest peasant out there why he'd
like to have a medal before going back on furlough. Because if he has a medal his girl will
like him better, and the other girls will run
after him, and he can use his medal to hook
other men's women away from under their
noses. That's the reason, the only reason.
The women sent us. No general could have
made us go if the women hadn't allowed us to
be stacked on the trains, if they had screamed
out that they would never look at us again if
we turned into murderers. Not a single man
would have gone off if they had sworn never
to give themselves to a man who has split open
other men's skulls and shot and bayoneted hu-

man beings. Not one man, I tell you, would
have gone. I didn't want to believe that they
could stand it like that. 'They're only pre-
tending,' I thought. 'They're just restrain-
ing themselves. But when the first whistle
blows, they'll begin to scream and tear us out
of the train, and rescue us.' *Once* they had
the chance to protect us, but all they cared
about was being in style—nothing else in the
world but just being in style."

He sank down on the bench again and sat
as though he were all broken up. His body
was shaken by a low weeping, and his head
rolled to and fro on his panting chest. A little circle of people had gathered behind his
back. The old landsturm corporal was standing beside the physician with four sentries
ready to intervene at a moment's notice. All
the windows in the officers' wing had lighted
up, and scantily clad figures leaned out, looking down into the garden curiously.

The sick man eagerly scrutinized the indifferent faces around him. He was exhausted.

His hoarse throat no longer gave forth a sound. His hand reached out for help to the Philosopher, who stood beside him, all upset.

The physician felt the right moment had come to lead him away.

"Come, Lieutenant, let's go to sleep," he said with a clumsy affectation of geniality. "That's the way women are once for all, and there's nothing to be done about it."

The physician wanted to go on talking and in conversing lure the sick man into the house unawares. But the very next sentence remained sticking in his throat, and he stopped short in amazement. The limp wobbling skeleton that only a moment before had sat there as in a faint and let himself be raised up by the physician and the Philosopher, suddenly jumped up with a jerk, and tore his arms away so violently that the two men who were about to assist him were sent tumbling up against the others. He bent over with crooked knees, staggering like a man carrying a heavy load on his back. His veins swelled, and he panted with fury:

"That's the way women are once for all, are they? Since when, eh? Have you never heard of the suffragettes who boxed the ears of prime ministers, and set fire to museums, and let themselves be chained to lamp-posts for the sake of the vote? For the sake of the vote, do you hear? But for the sake of their men? No. Not one sound. Not one single outcry!"

He stopped to take breath, overcome by a wild suffocating despair. Then he pulled himself together once more and with difficulty suppressing the sobs, which kept bringing a lump into his throat, he screamed in deepest misery like a hunted animal:

"Have you heard of one woman throwing herself in front of a train for the sake of her husband? Has a single one of them boxed the ears of a prime minister or tied herself to a railroad track for us? There wasn't one that had to be torn away. Not one fought for us or defended us. Not one moved a little finger for us in the whole wide world! They drove us out! They gagged us! They gave us the spur, like poor Dill. They sent us to murder, they sent us to die—for their vanity. Are you going to defend them? No! They must be pulled out! Pulled out like weeds, by the roots! Four of you together must pull the way we had to do with Dill. Four of you together! Then she'll have to come out. Are you the doctor? There! Do it to my head. I don't want a wife! Pull—pull her out!"

He flung out his arm and his fist came down like a hammer on his own skull, and his crooked fingers clutched pitilessly at the sparse growth of hair on the back of his head, until he held up a whole handful torn out by the roots, and howled with pain.

The doctor gave a sign, and the next moment the four sentries were on him, panting. He screamed, gnashed his teeth, beat about him, kicked himself free, shook off his assailants like burrs. It was not until the old cor-

poral and the doctor came to their assistance
that they succeeded in dragging him into the
house.

As soon as he was gone the people left the
garden. The last to go were the Mussulman
and the Philosopher. The Mussulman stopped
at the door, and in the light of the lantern
looked gravely down at his leg, which, in its
plaster cast, hung like a dead thing between
his two crutches.

"Do you know, Philosopher," he said, "I'd
much rather have this stick of mine. The
worst thing that can happen to one out there
is to go crazy like that poor devil. Rather off
with one's head altogether and be done with
it. Or do you think he still has a chance?"

The Philosopher said nothing. His round
good-natured face had gone ashen pale, and
his eyes were swimming with tears. He
shrugged his shoulders and helped his comrade up the steps without speaking. On en-
tering the ward they heard the banging of

doors somewhere far away in the house and a
muffled cry.

Then everything was still.   One by one the
lights went out in the windows of the officers'
wing.   Soon the garden lay like a bushy black
island in the river's silent embrace.   Only now
and then a gust of wind brought from the west
the coughing of the guns like a faint echo.

Once more a crunching sound was heard on
the gravel.   It was the four sentries marching back to the watch-house.   One soldier was
cursing under his breath as he tried to refasten
his torn blouse.   The others were breathing
heavily and were wiping the sweat from their
red foreheads with the backs of their hands.
The old corporal brought up the rear, his pipe
in the corner of his mouth, his head bent low.
As he turned into the main walk a bright sheet
of light lit up the sky, and a prolonged rumbling that finally sank into the earth with a
growl shook all the windows of the hospital.

The old man stood still and listened until
the rumbling had died away.   Then he shook

his clenched fist, and sent out a long curve of saliva from between his set teeth, and muttered in a disgust that came from the depths of his soul:

"Hell!"

BAPTISM OF FIRE

II

BAPTISM OF FIRE

THE company rested for half an hour at
the edge of the woods. Then Captain
Marschner gave the command to start. He
was pale, in spite of the killing heat, and he
turned his eyes aside when he gave Lieutenant
Weixler instructions that in ten minutes every
man should be ready for the march without
fail.

He had really forced his own hand in giving
the order. For now, he knew very well, there
could be no delay. Whenever he left Weixler
loose on the privates, everything went like
clock-work. They trembled before this lad of
barely twenty as though he were the devil incarnate. And sometimes it actually seemed to
the captain himself as though there were something uncanny about that overgrown, bony

figure. Never, by any chance, did a spark of warmth flash from those small, piercing eyes, which always mirrored a flickering unrest and gleamed as though from fever. The one young thing in his whole personality was the small, shy moustache above the compressed lips, which never opened except to ask in a mean, harsh way for some soldier to be punished. For almost a year Captain Marschner had lived side by side with him and had never yet heard him laugh, knew nothing of his family, nor from where he came, nor whether he had any ties at all. He spoke rarely, in brief, quick sentences, and brought out his words in a hiss, like the seething of a suppressed rage; and his only topic was the service or the war, as though outside these two things there was nothing else in the world worth talking about.

And this man, of all others, fate had tricked by keeping him in the hinterland for the whole first year of the war. The war had been going on for eleven months and a half, and Lieutenant Weixler had not yet seen an enemy.

At the very outset, when only a few miles across the Russian frontier, typhus had caught him before he had fired a single shot. Now at last he was going to face the enemy!

Captain Marschner knew that the young man had a private's rifle dragged along for his own use, and had sacrificed all his savings for special field-glasses in order to be quite on the safe side and know exactly how many enemy lives he had snuffed out. Since they had come within close sound of the firing he had grown almost merry, even talkative, impelled by a nervous zeal, like an enthusiastic hunter who has picked up the trail. The captain saw him going in and out among the massed men, and turned away, hating to see how the fellow plagued his poor weary men, and went at them precisely like a sheep dog gathering in the herd, barking shrilly all the while. Long before the ten minutes were up, the company would be in formation, Weixler's impatience guaranteed that. And then—then there would be no reason any more for longer delay, no further possibility of putting off the fatal decision.

Captain Marschner took a deep breath and looked up at the sky with wide-open eyes that had a peculiarly intent look in them. In the foreground, beyond the steep hill that still hid the actual field of battle from view, the invisible machine guns were beating in breathless haste; and scarcely a fathom above the edge of the slope small, yellowish-white packages floated in thick clusters, like snowballs flung high in the air—the smoke of the barrage fire through which he had to lead his men.

It was not a short way. Two kilometers still from the farther spur of the hill to the entrance of the communication trenches, and straight across open fields without cover of any kind. Assuredly no small task for a company of the last class of reservists, for respectable family men who had been in the field but a few hours, and who were only now to smell powder for the first time and receive their baptism of fire. For

Weixler, whose mind was set on nothing but
the medal for distinguished service, which he
wanted to obtain as soon as possible—for a
twenty-year-old fighting cock who fancied the
world rotated about his own, most important
person and had had no time to estimate the
truer values of life—for him it might be no
more than an exciting promenade, a new sting
to the nerves, a fine way of becoming thoroughly conscious of one's personality and
placing one's fearlessness in a more brilliant
light. Probably he had long been secretly de-
riding his old captain's indecision and had
cursed the last halt because it forced him to
wait another half hour to achieve his first deed
of heroism.

Marschner mowed down the tall blades of
grass with his riding whip and from time to
time glanced at his company surreptitiously.
He could tell by the way the men dragged
themselves to their feet with a sort of resistance, like children roused from sleep, that they
fully understood where they were now to go.

The complete silence in which they packed their bundles and fell into line made his heart contract.

Ever since the beginning of the war, he had been preparing himself for this moment without relax. He had brooded over it day and night, had told himself a thousand times that where a higher interest is at stake, the misery of the individual counts for nothing, and a conscientious leader must armor himself with indifference. And now he stood there and observed with terror how all his good resolutions crumbled, and nothing remained in him but an impassioned, boundless pity for these driven home-keepers, who prepared themselves with such quiet resignation. It was as if they were taking their life into their hands like a costly vessel in order to carry it into battle and cast it at the feet of the enemy, as though the least thing they owned was that which would soon be crashing into fragments.

His friends, among whom he was known as "uncle Marschner," would not have dared to suggest his sending a rabbit he had reared to the butcher or dragging a dog that had won his affection to the pound. And now he was to drive into shrapnel fire men whom he himself had trained to be soldiers and had had under his own eyes for months, men whom he knew as he did his own pockets. Of what avail were subtle or deep reflections now? He saw nothing but the glances of dread and beseeching that his men turned on him, asking protection, as though they believed that their captain could prescribe a path even for bullets and shells. And now was he to abuse their confidence? Was he to marshal these bearded children to death and not feel any emotion? Only two days before he had seen them surrounded by their little ones, saying good-bye to their sobbing wives. Was he to march on without caring if one or another of them was hit and fell over and rolled in agony in his blood? Whence was he to take the strength for such hardness of heart? From that higher interest? It had faded away. It was im-

palpable. It was too much a matter of mere
words, too much mere sound for him to think
that it could fool his soldiers, who looked forward to the barrage fire in dread, with home-
ward-turned souls.

Lieutenant Weixler, red-cheeked and radi-
ant, came and shouted in his face that the company was ready. It struck the captain like a
blow below the belt. It sounded like a challenge. The captain could not help hearing in
it the insolent question, "Well, why aren't you
as glad of the danger as I am?" Every drop
of Captain Marschner's blood rose to his temples. He had to look aside and his eyes wandered involuntarily up to the shrapnel clouds,
bearing a prayer, a silent invocation to those
senseless things up there rattling down so in-
discriminately, a prayer that they would teach
this cold-blooded boy suffering, convince him
that he was vulnerable.

But a moment later he bowed his head in
shame. His anger grew against the man who
had been able to arouse such a feeling in him.

"Thank you. Let the men stand at rest. I must look after the horses once more," he said in measured tones, with a forced composure that soothed him. He did not intend to be hustled, now less than ever. He was glad to see the lieutenant give a start, and he smiled to himself with quiet satisfaction at the indignant face, the defiant "Yes, sir," said in a voice no longer so loud and so clear, but coming through gnashed teeth from a contracted throat. The boy was for once in his turn to experience how it feels to be held in check. He was so fond of intoxicating himself with his own power at the cost of the privates, triumphing, as though it were the force of his own personality that lorded it over them and not the rule of the service that was always backing him.

Captain Marschner walked back to the woods deliberately, doubly glad of the lesson he had just given Weixler because it also meant a brief respite for his old boys. Perhaps a shell would hurtle down into the earth before their noses, and so these few minutes would save the lives of twenty men. Perhaps? It might turn out just the other way, too. Those very minutes—ah, what was the use of speculating? It was better not to think at all! He wanted to help the men as much as he could, but he could not be a savior to any of them.

And yet, perhaps? One man had just come rushing up to him from the woods. This one man he was managing to shelter for the present. He and six others were to stay behind with the horses and the baggage. Was it an injustice to detail this particular man? All the other non-commissioned officers were older and married. The short, fat man with the bow-legs even had six children at home. Could he justify himself at the bar of his conscience for leaving this young, unmarried man here in safety?

With a furious gesture the captain interrupted his thoughts. He would have liked best to catch hold of his own chest and give himself a sound shaking. Why could he not rid

himself of that confounded brooding and pon-
dering the right and wrong of things?
Was there any justice at all left here, here in
the domain of the shells that spared the worst
and laid low the best? Had he not quite made
up his mind to leave his conscience, his over-
sensitiveness, his ever-wakeful sympathy, and
all his superfluous thoughts at home along
with his civilian's clothes packed away in cam-
phor in the house where he lived in peace times?

All these things were part of the civil engi-
neer, Rudolf Marschner, who once upon a time
had been an officer, but who had returned to
school when thirty years old to exchange
the trade of war, into which he had wandered
in the folly of youth, for a profession that
harmonized better with his gentle, thoughtful
nature. That this war had now, twenty years
later, turned him into a soldier again was a
misfortune, a catastrophe which had overtaken
him, as it had all the others, without any fault
of his or theirs. Yet there was nothing to do
but to reconcile himself to it; and first of all he

had to avoid that constant hair-splitting. Why torment himself so with questions? Some man had to stay behind in the woods as a guard. The commander had decided on the young sergeant, and the young sergeant would stay behind. That settled it.

The painful thing was the way the fellow's face so plainly showed his emotion. His eyes moistened and looked at the captain in dog-like gratitude. Disgusting, simply disgusting! And what possessed the man to stammer out something about his mother? He was to stay behind because the service required it; his mother had nothing to do with it. She was safe in Vienna—and here it was war.

The captain told the man so. He could not let him think it was a bit of good fortune, a special dispensation, not to have to go into battle.

Captain Marschner felt easier the minute he had finished scolding the crushed sinner. His conscience was now quite clear, just as though it had really been by chance that he had placed the man at that post. But the feeling did not last very long. The silly fellow would not give up adoring him as his savior. And when he stammered, "I take the liberty of wishing you good luck, Captain," standing in stiff military attitude, but in a voice hoarse and quivering from suppressed tears, such fervor, such ardent devotion radiated from his wish that the captain suddenly felt a strange emptiness again in the pit of his stomach, and he turned sharply and walked away.

Now he knew. Now he could approximately calculate all the things Weixler had observed in him. Now he could guess how the fellow must have made secret fun of his sensitiveness, if this simple man, this mere carpenter's journeyman, could guess his innermost thoughts. For he had not spoken to him once—simply the night before last, at the entrainment in Vienna, he had furtively observed his leavetaking from his mother. How had the confounded fellow come to suspect that the wizened, shrunken little old hag whose skin, dried by long living, hung in a thousand loose folds from her cheek-bones, had made such an impression on his captain? The man himself certainly did not know how touching it looked when the tiny mother gazed up at him from below and stroked his broad chest with her trembling hand because she could not reach his face. No one could have betrayed to the soldier that since then, whenever his company commander looked at him, he could not help seeing the lemon-hued, thick-veined hand with its knotted, distorted fingers, which had touched the rough, hairy cloth with such ineffable love. And yet, somehow, the rascal had discovered that this hand floated above him protectingly, that it prayed for him and had softened the heart of his officer.

Marschner tramped across the meadow in rage against himself. He was as ashamed as though some one had torn a mask from his face. Was it as easy as that to see through him, then, in spite of all the trouble he took? He stopped to get his breath, hewed at the grass again with his riding whip, and cursed aloud. Oh, well, he simply couldn't act a part, couldn't step out of his skin suddenly, even though there was a world war a thousand times over. He used to let his nephews and nieces twist him round their fingers, and laughed good-naturedly when they did it. In a single day he could not change into a fire-eater and go merrily upon the man-hunt. What an utterly mad idea it was, too, to try to cast all people into the same mould! No one dreamed of making a soft-hearted philanthropist of Weixler; and he was supposed so lightly to turn straight into a blood-thirsty militarist. He was no longer twenty, like Weixler, and these sad, silent men who had been so cruelly uprooted from their lives were each of them far more to him than a mere rifle to be sent to the repair shop if broken, or to be indifferently discarded if smashed beyond repair. Whoever had looked on life from all sides and reflected upon it could not so easily turn into the mere soldier, like his lieutenant,

who had not been humanized yet, nor seen the
world from any point of view but the military
school and the barracks.

Ah, yes, if conditions still were as at the beginning of the war, when none but young fellows, happy to be off on an adventure, hal-
looed from the train windows. If they left
any dear ones at all behind, they were only
their parents, and here at last was a chance to
make a great impression on the old folks.
Then Captain Marschner would have held his
own as well as anyone, as well even as the strict
disciplinarian, Lieutenant Weixler, perhaps
even better. Then the men marched two or
three weeks before coming upon the enemy,
and the links that bound them to life broke off
one at a time. They underwent a thousand
difficulties and deprivations, until under the
stress of hunger and thirst and weariness they
gradually forgot everything they had left far
—far behind. In those days hatred of the
enemy who had done them all that harm
smouldered and flared higher every day, while

actual battle was a relief after the long period of passive suffering.

But now things went like lightning. Day before yesterday in Vienna still—and now, with the farewell kisses still on one's lips, scarcely torn from another's arms, straight into the fire. And not blindly, unsuspectingly, like the first ones. For these poor devils now the war had no secrets left. Each of them had already lost some relative or friend; each had talked to wounded men, had seen mutilated, distorted invalids, and knew more about shell wounds, gas grenades, and liquid fire than artillery generals or staff physicians had known before the war.

And now it was the captain's lot to lead precisely these clairvoyants, these men so rudely torn up by the roots—he, the retired captain, the civilian, who at first had had to stay at home training recruits. Now that it was a thousand times harder, now his turn had come to be a leader, and he dared not resist the task to which he was not equal. On the contrary, as a matter of decency, he had been forced to push his claims so that others who had already shed their blood out there should not have to go again for him.

A dull, impotent rage came over him when he stepped up in front of his men ranged in deep rows. They stared at his lips in breathless suspense. What was he to say to them? It went against him to reel off compliantly the usual patriotic phrases that forced themselves on one's lips as though dictated by an outside power. For months he had carried about the defiant resolve not to utter the prescribed *"dulce et decorum est pro patria mori,"* whatever the refusal might cost. Nothing was so repulsive to him as singing the praises of the sacrifice of one's life. It was a juggler's trick to cry out that some one was dying while inside the booth murder was being done.

He clenched his teeth and lowered his eyes shyly before the wall of pallid faces. The foolish, childlike prayer, "Take care of us!" gazed at him maddeningly from all those eyes. It drove him to sheer despair.

If only he could have driven them back to their own people and gone ahead alone! With a jerk he threw out his chest, fixed his eyes on a medal that a man in the middle of the long row was wearing, and said:

"Boys, we're going to meet the enemy now. I count upon each of you to do his duty, faithful to the oath you have sworn to the flag. I shall ask nothing of you that the interest of our fatherland and your own interest therefore and the safety of your wives and children do not absolutely require. You may depend upon that. Good luck! And now—forward, march!"

Without being conscious of it, he had imitated Weixler's voice, his unnaturally loud, studiedly incisive tone of command, so as to drown the emotion that fluttered in his throat. At the last words he faced about abruptly and without looking around tossed the final command over his shoulder for the men to deploy,

and with his head sunk upon his chest he began the ascent, taking long strides. Behind
him boots crunched and food pails clattered
against some other part of the men's accouter-
ment. Soon, too, there came the sound of the
gasping of heavily laden men; and a thick, suffocating smell of sweat settled upon the marching company.

Captain Marschner was ashamed. A real
physical nausea at the part he had just played
overcame him. What was there left for these
simple people to do, these bricklayers and engineers and cultivators of the earth, who, bent
over their daily tasks, had lived without vision
into the future—what was there left for them
to do when the grand folks, the learned people,
their own captain with the three golden stars
on his collar, assured them it was their duty
and a most praiseworthy thing to shoot Italian
bricklayers and engineers and farmers into
fragments? They went—gasping behind him,
and he—he led them on! Led them, against
his inner conviction, because of his pitiful

cowardice, and asked them to be courageous and contemptuous of death. He had talked them into it, had abused their confidence, had made capital of their love for their wives and children, because if he acted in the service of a lie, there was a chance of his continuing to live and even coming back home safe again, while if he stuck to the truth he believed in there was the certainty of his being stood up against a wall and shot.

He staked their lives and his own life on the throw of loaded dice because he was too cowardly to contemplate the certain loss of the game for himself alone.

The sun beat down murderously on the steep, treeless declivity. The sound of shells bursting off at a distance, of tattooing machine guns, and roaring artillery on their own side was now mingled with the howling sound of shots whizzing through the air and coming closer and closer. And still the top of the ridge had not been reached! The captain felt his breath fail him, stopped and raised his hand. The men were to get their wind back for a moment; they had been on the march since four o'clock that morning; they had done bravely with their forty-year-old legs. He could tell that by his own.

Full of compassion he looked upon the bluish red faces streaming with sweat, and gave a start when he saw Lieutenant Weixler approaching in long strides. Why could he no longer see that face without a sense of being attacked, of being caught at the throat by a hatred he could hardly control? He ought really to be glad to have the man at his side there. One glance into those coldly watchful eyes was sufficient to subdue any surge of compassion.

"With your permission, Captain," he heard him rasp out, "I'm going over to the left wing. A couple of fellows there that don't please me at all. Especially Simmel, the red-haired dog. He's already pulling his head in when a shrapnel bursts over there."

Marschner was silent. The red-haired dog

—Simmel? Wasn't that the red-haired end-man in the second line, the paper-hanger and upholsterer who had carried that exquisite little girl in his arms up to the last moment—until Weixler had brutally driven him off to the train? It seemed to the captain as though he could still see the children's astonished upward look at the mighty man who could scold their own father.

"Let him be, he'll get used to it by and by," he said mildly. "He's got his children on his mind and isn't in a hurry to make orphans of them. The men can't all be heroes. If they just do their duty."

Weixler's face became rigid. His narrow lips tightened again into that hard, contemptuous expression which the captain felt each time like the blow of a whip.

"He's not supposed to think of his brats now, but of his oath to the flag, of the oath he swore to his Majesty, his Commander-in-Chief! You just told them so yourself, Captain."

"Yes, yes, I know I did," Captain Marschner nodded absent-mindedly, and let himself slide down slowly on the grass. It was not surprising that this boy spoke as he did, but what *was* surprising was that twenty-five years ago, when he himself had come from the military academy all aglow with enthusiasm, the phrases "oath to the flag," "his Majesty, and Commander-in-Chief" had seemed to him, too, to be the sum and substance of all things. In those days he would have been like this lad and would have gone to war full of joyous enthusiasm. But now that he had grown deaf to the fanfaronade of such words and clearly saw the framework on which they were constructed, how was he to keep pace with the young who were a credulous echo of every speech they heard? How was he suddenly to make bold reckless blades of his excellent, comfortable Philistines, whom life had so thoroughly tamed that at home they were capable of going hungry and not snatching at treasures that were separated from them by only a thin partition of glass? What was the use of making the same demands upon the upholsterer Simmel as upon the young lieutenant, who had never striven for anything else than to be named first for fencing, wrestling, and courageous conduct? Have mercenaries ever been famous for their morals, or good solid citizens for their fearlessness? Can one and the same man be twenty and forty-five years old at the same time?

Crouching there, his head between his fists, the captain became so absorbed in these thoughts that he lost all sense of the time and the place, and the lieutenant's attempts to rouse him by passing by several times and hustling the men about loudly remained unsuccessful. But at last the sound of a horse's hoofs brought him back to consciousness. An officer was galloping along the path that ran about the hill half way from the top. On his head he wore the tall cap that marked him as a member of the general staff. He reined in his horse, asked courteously where the company was bound and raised his eyebrows when Captain Marschner explained the precise position they were to take.

"So that's where you're going?" he exclaimed, and his grimace turned into a respectful smile. "Well, I congratulate you! You're going into the very thickest of the lousy mess. For three days the Italians have been trying to break through at that point. I wouldn't hold you back for a moment! The poor devils there now will make good use of the relief. Good-bye and good luck!"

Gracefully he touched the edge of his cap. His horse cried out under the pressure of his spurs, and he was gone.

The captain stared after him as though dazed. "Well, I congratulate you!" The words echoed in his ears. A man, well mounted, thoroughly rested, pink and neat as though he had just come out of a band-box, meets two hundred fellowmen dedicated to death; sees them sweaty, breathless, on the very edge of destruction; knows that in another hour many a face now turned upon him curiously will lie in the grass distorted by pain or rigid in death—and he says, smiling, "Well, I congratulate you!" And he rides on and no shudder of awe creeps down his back, no shadow touches his forehead!

The meeting will fade from the man's memory without leaving a trace. At dinner that night nothing will remind him of the comrade whose hand, perhaps, he was the last one to press. To these chosen ones, who from their safe positions in the rear, drive the columns on into the fire, what matters a single company's march to death? And the miserable, red-haired upholsterer here was trembling, pulling back his head, tearing his eyes open mightily, as though the fate of the world depended upon whether he would ever again carry his little red-haired girl in his arms. To be sure, if one viewed the whole matter in the proper perspective—as a member of the general staff riding by, who kept his vision fixed on the aim, that is, the victory that sooner or later would be celebrated to the clinking of glasses—why, from that point of view Weixler was right! It must make him indignant to have events of such epic grandeur made ridiculous by such a chicken-hearted creature as Simmel and degraded into a doleful family affair.

"The poor devils there now!" A cold shiver ran down Marschner's back. The staff officer's words suddenly evoked a vision of the shattered, blood-soaked trench where the men, exhausted to the point of death, were yearning for him as for a redeemer. He arose, with a groan, seized by a grim, embittered hatred against this age. Not a single mesh in the net left open! Every minute of respite granted his own men was theft or even murder committed against the men out there. He threw up his arms and strode forward, determined to rest no more until he reached the trench that he and his company were to man and hold. His face was pale and careworn, and each time he caught the exasperating rasp of his lieutenant's voice from the other wing crying "Forward! Forward!" it was drawn by a tortured smile.

Suddenly he stood still. Into the rattle, the boom, the explosion of artillery there leaped suddenly a new tone. It rose clearly above the rest of the din, which had almost ceased to penetrate the consciousness. It approached with such a shrill sound, with such indescribable swiftness, with so fierce a threat, that the sound seemed to be visible, as though you could actually see a screaming semicircle rise in the air, bite its way to one's very forehead, and snap there with a short, hard, whiplike crack. A few feet away a little whirl of dust was puffed up, and invisible hail stones slapped rattling down upon the grass.

A shrapnel!

Captain Marschner looked round startled, and to his terror saw all the men's eyes fixed on him, as though asking his advice. A peculiar smile of shame and embarrassment hovered about their lips.

It was his business to set the men a good example, to march on carelessly without stopping or looking up. After all it made no difference what one did one way or the other. There was no possibility of running away or hiding. It was all a matter of chance. Chance was the one thing that would protect a man. So the thing to do was to go ahead as if not noticing anything. If there was only one man in the company who did not seem to care, the others would be put to shame and would mutually control each other, and then everything was won. He could tell by his own experience how the feeling of being watched on all sides upheld him. Had he been by himself, he might have thrown himself on the ground and tried to hide behind a stone no matter how small.

"Nothing but a spent shot! Forward, boys!" he cried, the thought of being a support to his men almost making him cheerful. But the words were not out of his mouth when other shots whizzed through the air. In spite of himself, his body twitched backward and his head sank lower between his shoulders. That made him stiffen his muscles and grind his teeth in rage. It was not the violence with which the scream flew toward him that made him twitch. It was the strange precision with which the circle of the thing's flight (exactly like a diagram at a lecture on artillery) curved in front of him. It was this unnatural feeling of perceiving a sound more with the eye than with the ear that made the will powerless.

Something had to be done to create the illusion of not being wholly defenseless.

"Forward, run!" he shouted at the top of his voice, holding his hands to his mouth to make a megaphone.

His men stormed forward as if relieved. The tension left their faces; each one was somehow busied with himself, stumbled, picked himself up, grasped some piece of equipment that was coming loose; and in the general snorting and gasping, the whistle of the approaching shells passed almost unobserved.

After a while it came to Captain Marschner's consciousness that some one was hissing into his left ear. He turned his head and
saw Weixler running beside him, scarlet in the
face.

"What is it?" he asked, involuntarily slow-
ing down from a run to a walk.

"Captain, I beg to announce that an example ought to be instituted! That coward Simmel is demoralizing the whole company. At
each shrapnel he yells out, 'Jesus, my
Savior,' and flings himself to the ground. He
is frightening the rest of the men. He ought
to be made an example of, a——"

A charge of four shrapnels whizzed into the
middle of his sentence. The screaming seemed
to have grown louder, more piercing. The
captain felt as though a monstrous, glittering
scythe were flashing in a steep curve directly
down on his skull. But this time he did not
dare to move an eyelash. His limbs contracted and grew taut, as in the dentist's chair
when the forceps grip the tooth. At the same

time, he examined the lieutenant's face closely, curious to see how he was taking the fire for which he had so yearned. But he seemed not to be noticing the shrapnels in the least. He was stretching his neck to inspect the left wing.

"There!" he cried indignantly. "D'you see, Captain? The miserable cur is down on his face again. I'll go for him!"

Before Marschner could hold him back, he had dashed off. But half-way he stopped, stood still, and then turned back in annoyance.

"The fellow's hit," he announced glumly, with an irritated shrug of his shoulders.

"Hit?" the captain burst out, and an ugly, bitter taste suddenly made his tongue cleave to the roof of his mouth. He observed the frosty calm in Weixler's features, the unsympathetic, indifferent look, and his hand started upward. He could have slapped him, his insensibility was so maddening and that careless "the fellow's hit" hurt so. The image of the dear little girl with the bright ribbon in her red curls flashed into his mind, and also the vision of a distorted corpse holding a child in its arms. As through a veil he saw Weixler hasten past him to catch up with the company, and he ran to where the two stretcher-bearers knelt next to something invisible.

The wounded man lay on his back. His flaming red hair framed a greenish grey face ghostly in its rigidity. A few minutes before Captain Marschner had seen the man still running—the same face still full of vitality—from heat and excitement. His knees gave way. The sight of that change, so incomprehensible in its suddenness, gripped at his vitals like an icy hand. Was it possible? Could all the life blood recede in the twinkling of an eye, and a strong, hale man crumble into ruins in a few moments? What powers of hell slept in such pieces of iron that between two breaths they could perform the work of many months of illness?

"Don't be frightened, Simmel!" the captain

stammered, supporting himself on the shoulder of one of the stretcher-bearers. "They'll carry you back to the baggage!" He forced the lie out with an effort, drawing a deep breath. "You'll be the first one to get back to Vienna now!" He wanted to add something about the man's family and the little girl with the red curls, but he could not get it over his lips. He dreaded a cry from the dying man for his dear ones, and when the mouth writhing with pain opened slowly, it sent an inner tremor through the captain. He saw the eyes open, too, and he shuddered at their glassy stare, which seemed no longer to fix itself upon any bodily thing but to be looking through all those present and seeking something at a distance.

Simmel's body writhed under the forcible examination of the doctor's hands. Incomprehensible gurgling sounds arose from his torn chest streaming with blood, and his breath blew the scarlet foam at his mouth into bursting bubbles.

"Simmel! What do you want, Simmel?" Marschner besought, bending low over the wounded man. He listened intently to the broken sounds, convinced that he would have to try to catch a last message. He breathed in relief when the wandering eyes at last found their way back and fastened themselves on his face with a look of anxious inquiry in them. "Simmel!" he cried again, and grasped his hand, which trembled toward the wound. "Simmel, don't you know me?"

Simmel nodded. His eyes widened, the corners of his mouth drooped.

"It hurts—Captain—hurts so!" came from the shattered breast. To the captain it sounded like a reproach. After a short rattling sound of pain he cried out again, foaming at the mouth and with a piercing shriek of rage: "It hurts! It hurts!" He beat about with his hands and feet.

Captain Marschner jumped up.

"Carry him back," he commanded, and without knowing what he did, he put his fingers into his ears, and ran after the company, which had already reached the top of the ridge. He ran pressing his head between his hands as in a vise, reeling, panting, driven by a fear, as though the wounded man's agonized cry were pursuing him with lifted axe. He saw the shrunken body writhe, the face that had so suddenly withered, the yellowish white of the eyes. And that cry: "Captain—hurts so!" echoed within him and clawed at his breast, so that when he reached the summit he fell down, half choked, as if the ground had been dragged from under his feet.

No, he couldn't do that sort of thing! He didn't want to go on with it. He was no hangman, he was incapable of lashing men on to their death. He could not be deaf to their woe, to that childlike whimpering which stung his conscience like a bitter reproach. He stamped on the ground defiantly. Everything in him arose in rebellion against the task that called him.

Below, the field of battle stretched far out,

cheerlessly grey.   No tree, no patch of green.
A stony waste—chopped up, crushed, dug inside out, no sign of life.   The communication
trenches, which started in the bottom of the
valley and led to the edge of the hill, from
which the wire entanglements projected,
looked like fingers spread out to grasp something and clawed deep into the throttled earth.
Marschner looked round again involuntarily.
Behind him the green slope descended steeply
to the little woods in which the baggage had
been left.   Farther behind the white highroad
gleamed like a river framed in colored meadows.   A short turn—and the greenness van-
ished!   All life succumbed, as though roared
down by the cannons, by the howling and
pounding that hammered in the valley like the
pulsating of a colossal fever.   Shell hole upon
shell hole yawned down there.   From time to
time thick, black pillars of earth leaped up and
for moments hid small parts of this desert
burned to ashes, where the cloven stumps of
trees, whittled as by pen-knives, stuck up like

a jeering challenge to the impotent imagination, a challenge to recognize in this field of death and refuse, the landscape it once had been, before the great madness had swept over it and sown it with ruins, leaving it like a dancing floor on which two worlds had fought for a loose woman.

And into this vale of hell he was now to descend! *Live* down there five days and five nights, he and his little company of the damned, spewed down into that place, their living bodies speared on the fishing hook, bait for the enemy!

All alone, with no one near to hear him, amid the fury of the bursting shrapnel, which fell up there as thick as rain in a thunderstorm, Captain Marschner gave himself up to his rage, his impotent rage against a world that had inflicted such a thing on him. He cursed and roared out his hatred into the deaf tumult; and then he sprang up when, far below, almost in the valley already, his men emerged followed by Lieutenant Weixler, who ran behind them like a butcher's helper driving oxen to the shambles. The captain saw them hurry, saw the clouds of the explosions multiply above their heads, and on the slope in front of him saw bluish-green heaps scattered here and there, like knapsacks dropped by the way, some motionless, some twitching like great spiders—and he rushed on.

He raced like a madman down the steep slope, scarcely feeling the ground under his feet, nor hearing the rattle of the exploding shells. He flew rather than ran, stumbled over charred roots, fell, picked himself up again and darted onward, looking neither to the right nor to the left, almost with closed eyes. Now and then, as from a train window, he saw a pale, troubled face flit by. Once it seemed to him he heard a man moaning for water. But he wished to hear nothing, to see nothing. He ran on, blind and deaf, without stopping, driven by the terror of that bad, reproachful, "Hurts so!"

Only once did he halt, as though he had stepped into a trap and were held fast in an iron vise. A hand stopped him, a grey, convulsed hand with crooked fingers. It stuck up in front of him as though hewn out of stone. He saw no face, nor knew who it was that held out that dead, threatening fist. All he knew was that two hours before, over there in the little piece of woods, that hand had still comfortably cut slices of rye bread or had written a last post-card home. And a horror of those fingers took hold of the captain and lent new strength to his limbs, so that he stormed onward in great leaps like a boy until, with throbbing sides and a red cloud before his eyes, he caught up with his company at last, way down in the valley at the entrance to the communication trenches.

Lieutenant Weixler presented himself in strictest military form and announced the loss of fourteen men. Marschner heard the ring of pride in his voice, like triumph over what had been achieved, like the rejoicing of a boy bragging of the first down on his lip and deepening the newly acquired dignity of a bass voice. What were the wounded men writhing on the slope above to this raw youth, what the red-haired coward with his whine, what the children robbed of their provider growing up to be beggars, to a life in the abyss, perhaps to a life in jail? All these were mere supers, a stage background for Lieutenant Weixler's heroism to stand out in relief. Fourteen bloody bodies lined the path he had trodden without fear. How should his eyes not radiate arrogance?

The captain hastened on, past Weixler. If only he did not have to see him, he told himself, if only he did not have to meet the contented gleam of the man's eyes. He feared his rage might master his reason and his tongue get beyond his control, and his clenched fist do its own will. But here he had to spare this man. Here Lieutenant Weixler was within his rights. He grew from moment to moment. His stature dwarfed the others. He swam upon the stream, while the others, weighed down by the burden of their riper humanity, sank like heavy clods. Here other laws obtained. The dark shaft in which they now reeled forward with trembling knees led to an island washed by a sea of death. .Whoever was stranded there dared not keep anything that he used in another world. The man who was master here was the one who had kept nothing but his axe and his fist. And he was the rich one upon whose superabundance the others depended. As Captain Marschner groped his way through the slippery trench in a daze, it became clearer and clearer to him that he must now hold on to his detested lieutenant like a treasure. Without him he would be lost.

He saw the traces of puddles of blood at his feet, and trod upon tattered, blood-soaked pieces of uniforms, on empty shells, rattling preserve tins, fragments of cannon balls. Yawning shell holes would open up suddenly, precariously bridged with half-charred boards.

Everywhere the traces of frenzied devastation
grinned, blackened remains of a wilderness of
wires, beams, sacks, broken tools, a disorder
that took one's breath away and made one
dizzy—all steeped in the suffocating stench
of combustion, powder smoke, and the pun-
gent, stinging breath of the ecrasite shells.
Wherever one stepped the earth had been lacerated by gigantic explosions, laboriously
patched up again, once more ripped open to
its very bowels, and leveled a second time, so
that one reeled on unconscious, as if in a hurricane.

Crushed by the weight of his impressions,
Captain Marschner crept through the trench
like a worm, and his thoughts turned ever more
passionately, ever more desperately to Lieutenant Weixler. Weixler alone could help him
or take his place, with that grim, cold energy
of his, with that blindness to everything which
did not touch his own life, or which was
eclipsed by the glowing vision of an Erich
Weixler studded with decorations and pro-

moted out of his turn. The captain kept looking about for him anxiously, and breathed
with relief each time the urgent, rasping voice
came to his ears from the rear.

The trench seemed never to be coming to
an end. Marschner felt his strength giving
way. He stumbled more frequently and
closed his eyes with a shudder at the criss-cross
traces of blood that precisely indicated the
path of the wounded. Suddenly he raised his
head with a jerk. A new smell struck him,
a sweetish stench which kept getting stronger
and stronger until at a curve of the trench
wall, which swung off to the left at this point
and receded semicircularly, it burst upon him
like a great cloud. He looked about, shaken
by nausea, his gorge rising. In a dip in the
trench he saw a pile of dirty, tattered uniforms
heaped in layers and with strangely rigid out-
lines. It took him some time to grasp the full
horror of that which towered in front of him.
Fallen soldiers were lying there like gathered
logs, in the contorted shapes of the last death

agony. Tent flaps had been spread over them, but had slipped down and revealed the grim, stony grey caricatures, the fallen jaws, the staring eyes. The arms of those in the top tier hung earthward like parts of a trellis, and grasped at the faces of those lying below, and were already sown with the livid splotches of corruption.

Captain Marschner uttered a short, belching cry and reeled forward. His head shook as though loosened from his neck, and his knees gave way so that he already saw the ground rising up toward him, when suddenly an unknown face emerged directly in front of him and attracted his attention, and gave him back his self-control. It was a sergeant, who was staring at him silently with great, fevered, gleaming eyes in a deathly pale face. For a moment the man stood as though paralyzed, then his mouth opened wide, he clapped his hands, and jumped into the air like a dancer, and dashed off, without thinking of a salute.

"Relief!" he shouted while running.

He came to a halt before a black hole in the trench wall, like the entrance to a cave, and bent down and shouted into the opening with a ring of indescribable joy in his voice—with a rejoicing that sounded as if it came through tears:

"Relief! Lieutenant! The relief party is here!"

The captain looked after him and heard his cry. His eyes grew moist, so touching was that childlike cry of joy, that shout from out of a relieved heart. He followed the sergeant slowly, and saw—as though the cry had awakened the dead—pallid faces peering from all corners, wounded men with blood-soaked bandages, tottering figures holding their rifles. Men streamed toward him from every direction, stared at him and with speechless lips formed the word "relief," until at length one of them roared out a piercing "hurrah," which spread like wildfire and found an echo in unseen throats that repeated it enthusiastically. Deeply shaken, Marschner bowed his head and swiftly drew his hand across his eyes when the commandant of the trench rushed toward him from the dugout.

Nothing that betokens life was left about the man. His face was ashen, his eyes like lamps extinguished, glazed and surrounded by broad blue rims. His lids were a vivid red from sleeplessness. His hair, his beard, his clothes were encased in a thick crust of mud, so that he looked as if he had just arisen from the grave. He gave a brief, military salute, then grasped the captain's hand with hysterical joy. His hand was cold as a corpse's and sticky with sweat and dirt. And most uncanny was the contrast between this skeleton hung with clothes, this rigid death-mask of a face, and the twitching, over-excited nervousness with which the lieutenant greeted their liberator.

The words leaped like a waterfall from his cracked lips. He drew Marschner into the dugout and pushed him, stumbling and groping as if dazzled, down on an invisible something meant for a seat and began to tell his tale. He couldn't stand still for a second. He hopped about, slapped his thighs, laughed with unnatural loudness, ran up and down trippingly, threw himself on the couch in the corner, asked for a cigarette every other minute, threw it away without knowing it after two puffs, and at once asked for another.

"I tell you, three hours more," he crowed blissfully, with affected gaiety, "—three? What am I talking about. *One* hour more, and it would have been too late. D'you know how many rounds of ammunition I've got left? Eleven hundred in all! Machine guns? Run down! Telephone? Smashed since last night already! Send out a party to repair it? Impossible! Needed every man in the trench! A hundred and sixty-four of us at first. Now I've got thirty-one, eleven of them wounded so that they can't hold a rifle. Thirty-one fellows to hold the trench with! Last night there were still forty-five of us when they attacked. We drove 'em to hell, of course, but fourteen of our men went again. We haven't had a chance to bury them yet. Didn't you see them lying out there?"

The Captain let him talk. He leaned his elbows on the primitive table, held his head between his hands, and kept silent. His eyes wandered about the dark, mouldy den, filled with the stench of a smoking little kerosene lamp. He saw the mildewed straw in the corner, the disconnected telephone at the entrance, an empty box of tinned food on which a crumpled map was spread out. He saw a mountain of rifles, bundles of uniforms, each one ticketed. And he felt how inch by inch, a dumb, icy horror arose within him and paralyzed his breathing, as though the earth overhead, upheld by only a thin scaffolding of cracked boards and threatening to fall at any moment, had already laid its intolerable weight upon his chest. And that prancing ghost, that giggling death's head, which only a week before perhaps had still been young, affected him like a nightmare. And the thought that now his turn had come to stick it out in that

sepulchral vault for five or six days or a week
and experience the same horrors that the man
there was telling about with a laugh intensi-
fied his discouragement into a passionate,
throbbing indignation which he could scarcely
control any more. He could have roared out,
could have jumped up, run out, and shouted
to mankind from the depths of his soul asking
why he had been tossed there, why he would
have to lie there until he had turned into carrion or a crazy man. How could he have let
himself be driven out there? He could not
understand it. He saw no meaning to it all,
no aim. All he saw was that hole in the earth,
those rotting corpses outside, and nearby, but
one step removed from all that madness, his
own Vienna as he had left it only two days before, with its tramways, its show windows, its
smiling people and its lighted theaters.
What madness to be crouching there waiting
for death with idiotic patience, to perish on
the naked earth in blood and filth, like a beast,
while other people, happy, clean, dressed up,

sat in bright halls and listened to music, and then nestled in soft beds without fear, without danger, guarded by a whole world, which would come down in indignation upon any who dared to harm a single hair of their heads. Had madness already stolen upon him or were the others mad?

His pulse raged as though his heart would burst if he could not relieve his soul by a loud shout.

At that very moment Lieutenant Weixler came bustling in, like the master of ceremonies at a ball. He stood stiff and straight in front of the captain, and announced that everything above was in readiness, that he had already assigned the posts and arranged the watches, and placed the machine guns. The captain looked at him and had to lower his eyes as if boxed on the ears by this tranquillity, which would suddenly wither his fury into a burning shame at himself.

Why did that man remain untouched by the great fear of death which impregnated the

very air here? How was it that he could give
orders and commands with the foresightedness
of a mature man, while he himself crept out
of sight like a frightened child and rebelled
against his fate with the senseless fury of an
animal at bay, instead of mastering fate as
befitted his age? Was he a coward? Was
he in the grip of a mean, paltry fear, was he
overcome by that wretched blindness of the
soul which cannot lift its vision beyond its own
ego nor lose sight of its ego for the sake of an
idea? Was he really so devoid of any sense
for the common welfare, so utterly ruled by
short-sighted selfishness, concerned with nothing but his bare, miserable existence?

No, he was not like that. He clung to his
own life no more than any other man. He
could have cast it away enthusiastically, and
without flying banners, without ecstasy, without the world's applause, had the hostile
trenches over there been filled with men like
Weixler, had the combat been against such
crazy hardness of soul, against catchwords

fattened with human flesh, against that whole,
cleverly built-up machine of force which drove
those whom it was supposed to protect to form
a wall to protect itself. He would have
hurled himself into the fight with bare fists,
unmindful of the bursting of shells, the moans
of the wounded. Oh no, he was not a coward.
Not what those two men thought. He saw
them wink scornfully and make fun of the unhappy old uncle of a reserve officer who sat
in the corner like a bundle of misery. What
did they know of his soul's bitterness? They
stood there as heroes and felt the glances of
their home upon them, and spoke words
which, upborne by the echo of a whole world,
peopled the loneliness with all the hosts of the
likeminded and filled their souls with the
strength of millions. And they laughed at a
man who was to kill without feeling hatred
and die without ecstasy, for a victory that was
nothing to him but a big force which achieved
its objects simply because it hit harder, not
because it had justice on its side or a fine and

noble aim. He had no cause to slink off,
humbled by their courage.

A cold, proud defiance heartened him, so
that he arose, strengthened suddenly, as if elevated by the superhuman burden that he alone
carried on his shoulders. He saw the strange
lieutenant still dancing about, hastily gathering up his belongings and stuffing them into
his knapsack. He heard him scold his orderly and bellow at him to hurry up, in between digging up fresh details, hideous epi-
sodes, from the combats of the past few days,
which Weixler devoured in breathless attention.

"What a question!" the commandant of the
trench exclaimed, laughing at his audience.
"Whether the Italians had heavy losses, too?
Do you think we let them pepper us like
rabbits? You can easily calculate what
those fellows lost in their eleven attacks if
we've melted down to thirty men without
crawling out of our trench. Just let them go

on like that a few weeks longer and they'll be at the end of their human material."

Captain Marschner had not wanted to listen. He stood bending over a map, but at the phrase, "human material," he started violently. It sounded like a taunt directed at his own thoughts, as if the two men had seen into him and had agreed with each other to give him a good lesson and show him how alone he was.

"Human material!"

In a trench, filled with the stench of dead bodies, shaken by the impact of the shells, stood two men, each himself a stake in the game, and while the dice were still being tossed for their very bones, they talked of— human material! They uttered those ruthless, shameful words without a shadow of indignation, as though it were natural for their living bodies to be no more than a gambler's chips in the hands of men who arrogated to themselves the right to play the game of gods. Without hesitating they laid their one, irrevocable life at the feet of a power that could not prove whether it had known how to place the stakes rightly except by their dead bodies. And the men who were speaking that way were officers! So where was there a gleam of hope?

Out there, among the simple men, perhaps, the plain cannon fodder? They were now crouching resignedly in their places, thinking of home and each of them still feeling himself a man. He was drawn to his men, to their dull, silent sadness, to their true greatness, which without pathos and without solemnity, in everyday clothes, as it were, patiently awaited the hero's death.

Outside the dugout stood the remnants of the relieved company ready for the march, always two men abreast with a dead comrade on a tent canvas between them. A long procession, profoundly stirring in its silent expectancy, into which the hissing and crackling of shrapnel and the thunder of grenades fell like a warning from above to those who still had

their lives.   Bitterly, Marschner clenched his
fist at this insatiableness.

At that moment the pale sergeant stepped
in front of the place where the dead had been
piled and frightened Marschner out of his
thoughts.

"Captain, I beg to announce that beside the
fourteen dead there are three seriously
wounded men who can't walk—Italians.   I
have no bearers left for them."

"We'll leave them to you as a souvenir," the
trench commandant, who was just leaving the
dugout with Weixler, laughed in his maunder-
ing way.   "You can have them dug in at night
up there among the communication trenches,
Captain.   When it gets dark, the Italians direct their barrage fire farther back, and give
you a chance to climb out.   To be sure, they
won't lie in peace there under the earth very
long, because the shells rip everything open
right away again.   I've had to have my poor
ensign buried three times over already."

"How did they get in here anyhow?" Weixler asked, pushing himself forward. "Did you have a fight in the trench?"

The other lieutenant shook his head proudly. "I should rather say not. The gentlemen never got as far as that. These three tried to cut the wire entanglements night before last, but our machine gun man caught 'em at it and his iron spatter spoiled their little game. Well, there they lay, of course, right under our very noses and they had on the loveliest shoes of bright yellow. My men begrudged 'em those shoes. There—" he ended, pointing with his finger at the feet of the pale sergeant— "there you see one pair. But we'll have to start now. March, sergeant! My respects, Captain. The Italians'll open their eyes when they come over to-night to finish us off comfortably and a hundred and fifty rifles go off and two brand-new bullet squirters. Ha-ha! Sorry I can't be here to see it! Good-by, little man! Good luck!" Humming a merry popular song he followed his men—without looking back, without even observing that

Marschner accompanied him a little on his way.

Gaily, as though on a Sunday picnic, the men started on the way, which led over the terrible field of shards and ruins and the steep, shot-up hill. What hells they must have endured there, in that mole's gallery! The captain remained standing and heaved a deep sigh. It was as if that long, grey column slowly winding its way through the trench were carrying away the last hope. The back of the last soldier, growing smaller and smaller, was the world. The captain's eyes clung greedily to that back and measured fearfully the distance to the corner of the trench from which he must lose sight of it forever. There was still time to call out a greeting, and by running very fast one might still catch up and hand over a letter.

Then the last medium disappeared—the last possibility of dividing the world into two halves. And his yearning recoiled before the

endless space it had to bridge—and there was
nothing else to bridge it but his yearning.

Marschner sank into himself as he stood deserted in the empty trench. He felt as though
he had been hollowed out, and looked about
for help, and his eyes clung to the depression
from which the corpses had now been lifted.
Only the three Italians were lying there, the
life already gone from them. The one showed
his face, his mouth was still wide open as for a
cry, and his hands dug themselves, as though
to ward off pain, into his unnaturally swollen
body. The other two lay with their knees
drawn up and their heads between their arms.
The naked feet with their grey convulsed toes
stared into the communication trench like
things robbed, with a mute accusal. There
was a remoteness about these dead bodies, a
loneliness, an isolation about their bared feet.
A tangled web of memories arose, a throng of
fleeting faces glimmered in the captain's soul
—gondoliers of Venice, voluble cabbies, a
toothless inn-keeper's wife at Posilipo. Two

trips on a vacation in Italy drove an army of
sorrowing figures through his mind. And
finally another figure appeared in that ghostly
dance of death, his own sister, sitting in a concert hall in Vienna, care-free, listening to
music, while her brother lay somewhere
stretched out on the ground, rigid in death,
an enemy's corpse just to be kicked aside.

Shuddering, the captain hastened back down
the trench, as though the three dead men were
pursuing him noiselessly on their naked soles.
When he reached his own men at last, he felt
as if he had arrived at a harbor of safety.

The shells were now falling so thick that
there was not a moment's pause between the
explosions, and all sounds merged into a single, equal, rolling thunder, which made the
earth tremble like the hull of a ship. But there
was a particularly sharp crashing and splin-
tering from one shot that hit the trench
squarely and whirled the coverings above in
all directions. A few minutes later two
groaning men dragged down a corpse, leaned

it against the trench wall, and climbed back
to their posts through the narrow shaft.
Marschner saw his sergeant get up and move
his lips—then a soldier in the corner arose and
took up his rifle and followed the two others
heavily. It was all so comfortless, so unmer-
cifully businesslike, precisely as when "Next!"
breaks into the monotony of the practising in
the yard of the barracks, only with the difference that a little group at once gathered about
the dead man, drawn by that shy curiosity
which irresistibly attracts simple folk to
corpses and funerals. Most of the men expected the same of him—he saw it in their
eyes—that he, too, would go over and pay a
last tribute of respect to the dead. But he
did not want to. He was absolutely determined not to learn the fallen man's name. He
was bent upon practising self-mastery at last
and remaining indifferent to all small hap-
penings. So long as he had not seen the dead
man's face nor heard his name, only a man
had fallen in battle, one of the many thou-

sands. If he kept his distance and did not bend over each individual and did not let a definite fate come to his notice, it was not so hard to remain indifferent.

Stubbornly he walked over to the second shaft leading to the top and for the first time observed that it had grown quite silent up above. There was no longer any screaming or bursting. This silence came upon the deafening din like a paralyzing weight and filled space with a tense expectancy that flickered in all eyes. He wanted to rid himself of this oppression and crept through the crumbling shaft up to the top.

The first thing he saw was Weixler's curved back. He was holding his field-glass glued to his eyes under cover of a shooting shield. The others were also standing as if pasted to their posts, and there was something alarming in the motionlessness of their shoulder blades. All at once a twitching ran through the petrified row. Weixler sprang back, jostled against the captain, and cried out: "They are coming!" Then he stormed to the shaft and blew the alarm whistle.

Marschner stared after him helplessly. He walked with hesitating steps to the shield and looked out upon the wide, smoke-covered field, which curved beyond the tangle of wires, grey, torn, blood-flecked, like the bloated form of a gigantic corpse. Far in the background the sun was sinking. Its great copper disc already cut in half by the horizon seemed to be growing out of the ground. And against that dazzling background black silhouettes were dancing like midges under a microscope, like Indians swinging their tomahawks. They were still mere specks. Sometimes they disappeared entirely and then leaped high, and came nearer, their rifles wriggling in the air life the feet of a polyp. Gradually their cries became audible and swelled louder and louder like the far barking of dogs. When they called "Avanti!" it was a piercing cry, and when the call "Coraggio!" went through their lines, it changed to a dull, thunderous roll.

The entire company now stood close-packed up against the slope of the trench, their faces as of stone, restrained, pale as chalk, with lipless mouths, each man's gun in position—a single beast of prey with a hundred eyes and arms.

"Don't shoot! Don't shoot! Don't shoot!" Lieutenant Weixler's voice yelled without pause through the trench. His command seemed to lay its grasp on every throat and to hold the fingers moveless that greedily clasped the triggers. The first hand grenade flew into the trench. The captain saw it coming, then saw a man loosen from the mass, reel toward the dugout with outstretched arms, bending over, a veil of blood covering his face. Then— at last!—it was a relief—came the beating of the machine guns, and at once the rifles went off, too, like the raging of an angry pack. A cold, repulsive greed lay on all faces. Some of the men cried out aloud in their hate and rage when new groups emerged out there behind the thinning rows. The barrels of the rifles glowed with heat—and still the rumbling cries of "Coraggio!" came nearer and nearer.

As though in a frenzy of insanity, the silhouettes hopped about out there, sprang into the air, fell, and rolled over each other, as though the war dance had only just reached the climax of its paroxysm.

Then Captain Marschner observed the man next to him let his rifle sink for a moment and with hasty, shaking hands insert the bayonet into the smoking barrel. The captain felt as though he were going to vomit. He closed his eyes in dizziness and leaned against the trench wall, and let himself glide to the earth. Was he to—to see—that? Was he to see men being murdered right alongside of him? He tore his revolver from his pocket, emptied it, and threw it away. Now he was defenseless. And suddenly he grew calm and rose to his feet, elevated by a wonderful composure, ready to let himself be butchered by one of those panting beasts who were storming on, chased by the blind fear of death. He wanted to die like a man, without hatred, without rage, with clean hands.

A hoarse roar, a frightful, dehumanized cry almost beside him wrenched his thoughts back into the trench. A broad stream of light and fire, travelling in a steep curve, flowed blindingly down beside him and sprayed over the shoulder of the tall pock-marked tailor of the first line. In the twinkling of an eye the man's entire left side flared up in flames. With a howl of agony he threw himself to the ground, writhed and screamed and leaped to his feet again, and ran moaning up and down like a living torch, until he broke down, half-charred, and twitched, and then lay rigid. Captain Marschner saw him lying there and smelt the odor of burned flesh, and his eyes involuntarily strayed to his own hand on which a tiny, white spot just under his thumb reminded him of the torments he had suffered in his boyhood from a bad burn.

At that moment a jubilant hurrah roared through the trench, rising from a hundred relieved throats. The attack had been repulsed! Lieutenant Weixler had carefully taken aim at the thrower of the liquid fire and hit at the first shot. The liquid fire had risen up like a fountain from the falling man's stiffening hand and rained down on his own comrades. Their decimated lines shrank back suddenly before the unexpected danger and they fled pell-mell, followed by the furious shots from all the rifles.

The men fell down as if lifeless, with slack faces and lusterless eyes, as though some one had turned off the current that had fed those dead creatures with strength from some unknown source. Some of them leaned against the trench wall white as cheese, and held their heads over, and vomited from exhaustion. Marschner also felt his gorge rising and groped his way toward the dugout. He wanted to go into his own place now and be alone and somehow relieve himself of the despair that held him in its grip.

"Hello!" Lieutenant Weixler cried unexpectedly through the silence, and bounded over to the left where the machine guns stood.

The captain turned back again, mounted the ladder, and gazed out into the foreground of the field. There, right in front of the wire-entanglements, kneeled an Italian. His left arm was hanging down limp, and his right arm was raised beseechingly, and he was crawling toward them slowly. A little farther back, half hidden by the kneeling man, something kept stirring on the ground. There three wounded men were trying to creep toward their own trench, pressing close to the ground. One could see very clearly how they sought cover behind corpses and now and then lay motionless so as to escape discovery by the foe. It was a pitiful sight—those God-forsaken creatures surrounded by death, each moment like an eternity above them, yet clinging with tooth and nail to their little remnant of life.

"Come on! Isn't there a rope somewhere?" an old corporal called down into the trench. "I'm sorry for the poor devil of an Italian. Let's pull him in!"

The machine guns interrupted him. The kneeling man beside the wires listened, started as if to run, and fell upon his face. The earth behind him rose in dust from the bullets and the others beyond raised themselves like snakes, then all three gave a short leap forward and—lay very still.

For a moment Captain Marschner stood speechless. He opened his lips, but no sound came from his throat. At last his tongue obeyed him and he yelled, with a mad choking fury in his voice:

"Lieutenant Weixler!"

"Yes, sir," came back unconcernedly.

Captain Marschner ran toward the lieutenant with clenched fists and scarlet face.

"Did you fire?" he panted, breathless.

The lieutenant looked at him in astonishment, placed his hands against the seams of his trousers and replied with perfect formality:

"I did, sir."

Marschner's voice failed him again for a moment. His teeth chattered. His whole body trembled as he stammered:

"Aren't you ashamed of yourself? A soldier doesn't fire at helpless, wounded men. Remember that!"

Weixler went white.

"I beg to inform you, Captain, that the one who was near our trench was hiding the others from us. I couldn't spare him." Then, with a sudden explosion of anger, he added defiantly: "Besides, I thought we had quite enough hungry mouths at home as it is."

The captain jumped at him like a snapping dog and stamped his foot and roared:

"I'm not interested in what you think. I forbid you to shoot at the wounded! As long as I am commanding officer here every wounded man shall be held sacred, whether he

tries to get to us or to return to the enemy.
Do you understand me?"

The lieutenant drew himself up haughtily.

"In that case I must take the liberty, sir, of
begging you to hand me that order in writing. I consider it my duty to inflict as much
injury upon the enemy as possible. A man
that I let off to-day may be cured and come
back two months later and perhaps kill ten of
my comrades."

For a moment the two men stood still, staring at each other as though about to engage in
mortal combat. Then Marschner nodded his
head almost imperceptibly, and said in a tone-
less voice:

"You shall have it in writing."

He swung on his heel and left. Colored
spheres seemed to dance before his eyes, and
he had to summon all his strength to keep his
equilibrium. When at last he reached the
dugout, he fell on the box of empty tins as
if he had been beaten. His hatred changed
slowly into a deep, embittered sense of dis-

couragement. He knew perfectly well that he
was in the wrong. Not at the bar of his conscience! His conscience told him that the
deed the lieutenant had done was cowardly
murder. But he and his conscience had nothing to say here. They had happened to stray
into this place and would have to stay in the
wrong. What was he to do? If he gave the
order in writing, he would afford Weixler his
desired opportunity of pushing himself forward and invite an investigation of his own
conduct. He begrudged the malicious creature that triumph. Perhaps it were better to
make an end of the whole business by going
to the brigade staff and telling the exalted
gentlemen there frankly to their faces that he
could no longer be a witness to that bloody
firing, that he could not hunt men like wild
beasts, no matter what uniform they happened
to wear. Then, at least, this playing at hide
and seek would end. Let them shoot him, if
they wanted to, or hang him like a common

felon. He would show them that he knew how to die.

He walked out into the trench firmly, and ordered a soldier to summon Lieutenant Weixler. Now it was so clear within him and so calm. He heard the hellish shooting that the Italians were again directing at the trench and went forward slowly like a man out promenading.

"They're throwing heavy mines at us now, Captain," the old corporal announced, and looked at Marschner in despair. But Marschner went by unmoved. All that no longer mattered to him. The lieutenant would take over the command. That was what he was going to tell him. He could hardly await the moment to relieve himself of the responsibility.

As Weixler delayed coming, he crept up through the shaft to the top.

The man's small, evil eyes flew to meet him and sought the written order in his hand. The captain acted as though he did not notice the question in his look, and said imperiously:

"Lieutenant, I turn the command of the company over to you until——"

A short roar of unheard-of violence cut short his speech. He had the feeling, "That will hit me," and that very instant he saw something like a black whale rush down in front of his eyes from out of the heavens and plunge head foremost into the trench wall behind him. Then a crater opened up in the earth, a sea of flame that raised him up and filled his lungs with fire.

On slowly recovering his consciousness he found himself buried under a huge mound of earth, with only his head and his left arm free. He had no feeling in his other limbs. His whole body had grown weightless. He could not find his legs. Nothing was there that he could move. But there was a burning and burrowing that came from somewhere in his brain, scorched his forehead, and made his tongue swell into a heavy, choking lump.

"Water!" he moaned. Was there no one there who could pour a drop of moisture into the burning hollow of his mouth? No one at all? Then where was Weixler? He must be near by. Or else—was it possible that Weixler was wounded too? Marschner wanted to jump up and find out what had happened to Weixler—he wanted to——

Like an overburdened steam-crane his left hand struggled toward his head, and when he at last succeeded in pushing it under his neck, he felt with a shudder that his skull offered no resistance and his hand slid into a warm, soft mush, and his hair, pasty with coagulated blood, stuck to his fingers like warm, moist felt.

"Dying!" went through him with a chill. To die there—all alone. And Weixler? He had to find out what had happened to—happened to——

With a superhuman effort he propped his head up on his left hand high enough to have a view of a few paces along the trench. Now he saw Weixler, with his back turned, leaning on his right side against the trench wall, standing there crookedly, his left hand pressed against his body, his shoulders hunched as if he had a cramp. The captain raised himself a little higher and saw the ground and a broad, dark shadow that Weixler cast. Blood? He was bleeding? Or what? Surely that was blood. It couldn't be anything but blood. And yet it stretched out so peculiarly and drew itself like a thin, red thread up to Weixler, up to where his hand pressed his body as though he wanted to pull up the roots that bound him to the earth.

The captain *had* to see! He pulled his head farther out from under the mound—and uttered a hoarse cry, a cry of infinite horror. The wretched man was dragging his entrails behind him!

"Weixler!" burst from him in a shudder of compassion.

The man turned slowly, looked down at Marschner questioningly, pale, sad, with frightened eyes. He stood like that only the fraction of a second, then he lost his balance, reeled, and fell down, and was lost from the captain's circle of vision. Their glances scarcely had time to cross, the pallid face had merely flitted by. And yet it stood there, remained fixed in the air, with a mild, soft, plaintive expression about the narrow lips, an unforgettable air of gentle anxious resignation.

"He is suffering!" flashed through Marschner. "He is suffering!"—it exulted him. And a glow suffused his pallor. His fingers, sticky with blood, seemed to caress the air, until his head sank backward, and his eyes broke.

The first soldiers who penetrated the towering mound of earth to where he lay found him dead. But in spite of his ghastly wound, a contented, almost happy smile hovered about his lips.

THE VICTOR

III

THE VICTOR

ON the big square before the old court-house, which now served as regimental headquarters and bore the magic letters A. O. K. as a sort of cabalistic sign on its front, a military band played every afternoon from three to four at command of His Excellency. This little diversion was meant to compensate the civilian population for the many inconveniences that the quartering of several hundreds of staff officers and a number of lesser officers inevitably brought upon them. Then, too, according to His Excellency, such an institution helped considerably to promote the popularity of the army and inspire patriotism in school children and the masses. In the interest of the right conduct of the war the strict commander deemed it highly essential to foster a right attitude in the public and to encourage friendly relations between military and civilian authorities—while fully preserving his own privileges. It was essential to a successful continuation of the war. Incidentally, the fact that the staff officers, with His Excellency at their head, usually took their black coffee at just about this time had helped a good deal to bring about these afternoon concerts.

It was indeed delightful to sit in the shade of the centenarian plane-trees, whose intertwining branches overarched the entire square like the nave of a cathedral. The autumn sun cast a dull glow on the walls of the houses round about, and shed golden rings through the thick foliage on the small round tables arrayed in long rows in front of the coffee-house. There was a reserved row for the staff officers set in snowy linens, with little flower vases and fresh crisp cakes, which the sergeant of the commissary brought punctually at three o'clock every day from the field bakery, where they had been baked with particular care under the personal supervision of the chef especially for His Excellency and staff.

It was a beautiful gay picture of lively, varied metropolitan life that surged about the music pavilion.   Every one seemed as joyous and carefree as on the Graben in Vienna on a sunny spring Sunday in times of undisturbed peace.   The children crowded around the orchestra, beat the measure, and applauded enthusiastically after every piece.   The streets leading into the square were filled with giggling girls and students wearing bright caps; while the *haute-volée,* the wives of the resident officials and merchants, sat in the confectioner's shop on the square, eagerly awaiting an opportunity to show their righteous indignation at the daring millinery, transparent hose, and little more than knee-length skirts of a certain class of women who had forced their way into the town and, despite all protests and orders, were shamelessly plying their trade in broad daylight.

But the chief tone was given by the transient officers. Whether on furlough or on their way back to the front, they all had to pass through this town, and enjoyed in deep draughts this first or last day of freedom. Besides, if anything was needed at the front—horse-shoe nails, saddle-soap, sanitary appliances, or bottled beer—this first little "big town" was the quickest, most convenient place to buy it in. An unlucky or an unpopular man merely received a commendation for his bravery, and that settled him. But the man who enjoyed his commanding officer's favor was given the preference to do the shopping here as a reward. And an amazing ingenuity developed in discovering immediate necessities. A secret arithmetical relation undeniably existed between the consumption of charcoal, axle grease, etc., by individual troop divisions and the distance of their outposts from this favorite provisioning station.

Of course, the pleasure did not last long. There was just enough time for a hot tub-bath, for showing off one's best newly-pressed uniform once or twice on the main streets, for taking two meals at a table spread with a tablecloth, and for spending a short night in a comfortable bed—with, or, if the man could not help it, without caresses—and then off again, depressed and irritable, off to the maddeningly overcrowded railroad station, back to the front, into the damp trench or the sunbaked block house.

The greed of life in these young officers, who promenaded, hungry-eyed, through the town, the racing of their blood, like a diver who fills his lungs full in one second, had gradually infected the entire, boresome little place. It tingled, it foamed, it enriched itself and became frivolous; it could not get enough sensations, now that it stood in the center of world activities and had a claim upon real events.

Close-packed, the crowd surged past the music in holiday attire and holiday mood on this ordinary week-day, quivering to the rhythm of the Blue Danube Waltz, which the

orchestra was playing catchingly, with a roll
of drums and a clash of cymbals. The whole
spectacle brought to mind the goings-on behind the scenes in a huge playhouse during
the performance of a tragedy with choruses
and mob scenes. Nothing was seen or heard
here of the sanguinary piece being enacted at
the front. The features of the actors re-
laxed, they rested, or threw themselves into
the gay hubbub, heartily glad not to know how
the tragedy was progressing; exactly as real
actors behind the scenes fall back into their
unprofessional selves until they get their next
cue.

Sitting in the shade of the old trees, over
coffee and cigars, comfortably watching these
doings, one might easily be deluded into thinking that the drama taking place at the front
was nothing but a jolly spectacular play.
From this point of view the whole war showed
up like a life-giving stream that washes orches-
tras ashore, brings wealth and gaiety to the
people, is navigated by promenading officers,

and directed by portly, comfortable generals. No suggestion of its bloody side, no roar of artillery reaching your ears, no wounded soldier dragging in his personal wretchedness and so striking a false note in the general jollification.

Of course, it had not always been like that. In the first days, when the daily concert still had the charm of novelty, all the regular, emergency and reserve hospitals in the neighborhood had poured their vast number of convalescents and slightly wounded men into the square. But that lasted only two days. Then His Excellency summoned the head army physician to a short interview and in sharp terms made it clear to the crushed culprit what an unfavorable influence such a sight would have upon the public, and expressed the hope that men wearing bandages, or maimed men, or any men who might have a depressing effect on the general war enthusiasm, should henceforth remain in the hospitals.

He was not defrauded of his hope. No disagreeable sight ever again marred his pleasure when, with his favorite Havana between his teeth, he gazed past the long row of his subordinates out on the street. No one ever went by without casting a shy, deferential sideglance at the omnipotent director of battles, who sat there like any other ordinary human being, sipping his coffee, although he was the celebrated General X, unlimited master of hundreds of thousands of human lives, the man the papers liked to call the "Victor of ——." There was not a human being in the town whose fate he could not have changed with one stroke of his pen. There was nothing he could not promote or destroy as he saw fit. His good will meant orders for army supplies and wealth, or distinction and advancement; his ill will meant no prospects at all, or an order to march along the way that led to certain death.

Leaning back comfortably in the large wicker chair, a chair destined in all likelihood some day to become an object of historic interest, the Powerful One jested gaily with the wife of his adjutant. He pointed to the street, where the crowds surged in the brilliant sunshine, and said with a sort of satisfied, triumphant delight in his tone:

"Just look! I should like to show this picture to our pacifists, who always act as though war were nothing but a hideous carnage. You should have seen this hole in peace times. It was enough to put you to sleep. Why, the porter at the corner is earning more to-day than the biggest merchant used to earn before the war. And have you noticed the young fellows who come back from the front? Sunburnt, healthy and happy! Most of them before the war were employed in offices. They held themselves badly and were dissipated and looked cheesy. I assure you, the world has never been so healthy as it is now. But if you look at your newspapers, you read about a world-catastrophe, about a blood-drained Europe, and a whole lot of other stuff."

He raised his bushy white eyebrows until

they reached the middle of his bulging forehead, and his small, piercing black eyes skimmed observantly over the faces of those present.

His Excellency's pronouncement was a suggestion to the others and was immediately taken up. At every table the conversation grew animated, the benefits of the war were told over, and the wits cracked jokes at the expense of the pacifists. There was not a single man in the whole assemblage who did not owe at least two blessings to the war: financial independence and such munificence of living as only much-envied money magnates have allotted to them in times of peace. Among this circle of people the war wore the mask of a Santa Claus with a bag full of wonderful gifts on his back and assignments for brilliant careers in his hand. To be sure here and there a gentleman was to be seen wearing a crêpe-band on his sleeve for a brother or a brother-in-law who, as officer, had seen that other aspect of the war, the Gorgon's face.

Yet the Gorgon's face was so far away, more than sixty miles in a bee-line, and an occasional excursion in its vicinity was an exciting little adventure, a brief titillation of the nerves. Inside an hour the automobile raced back to safety, back to the bath-tub, and you promenaded asphalt streets again in shining pumps. So, who would refrain from joining in the hymn of praise to His Excellency?

The mighty man contentedly listened a while longer to the babel of voices aroused by what he had said, then gradually sank back into his reflections, and gazed ahead of him seriously.   He saw the sunbeams sifting through the thick foliage and glittering on the crosses and stars that covered the left half of his chest in three close rows.   It was a magnificent and complete collection of every decoration that the rulers of four great empires had to bestow upon a man for heroism, contempt of death, and high merit.   There was no honor left for the Victor of —— still to aspire to.   And only eleven short months of war had cast all that at his feet. It was the harvest of but a single year of war. Thirty-nine years of his life had previously gone in the service in tedious monotony, in an eternal struggle with sordid everyday cares. He had worn himself out over all the exigencies of a petty bourgeois existence, like a poor man ashamed of his poverty, making pathetic efforts to conceal a tear in his clothes and always seeing the telltale hole staring out from under the covering. For thirty-nine years he had never swerved from disciplining himself to abstemiousness, and there was much gold on his uniform, but very little in his pocket. As a matter of fact, he had been quite ready for some time to quit. He was thoroughly tired of the cheap pleasure of tyrannizing over the young officers on the drill ground.

But then the miracle occurred! Over night the grouchy, obscure old gentleman changed into a sort of national hero, a European celebrity. He was "the Victor of ——!" It was like in a fairy tale, when the good fairy

appears and frees the enchanted prince from
his hideous disguise, and he emerges in his
glowing youth, surrounded by knights and
lackeys, and enters his magnificent castle.

To be sure the miracle had not brought the
general the glow of youth. But it put elas-
ticity into him. The eventful year had given
him a shaking up, and his veins pulsed with the
joy of life and the energy for work of a man
in his prime. It was as a sovereign that he
sat there in the shadow of the plane-trees, with
good fortune sparkling on his chest and a city
lying at his feet. Nothing, not a single thing,
was lacking to make the fairy tale perfect.

In front of the coffee-house, guarded by two
sturdy corporals, rested the great grey beast,
with the lungs of a hundred horses in its chest,
awaiting the cranking-up to rush its master
off to his castle high above town and valley.
Where were the days when, with his general's
stripes on his trousers, he took the street-car
to his home, befitting his station in life, a six-
room apartment that was really a five-room

apartment plus a closet? Where was all that? Centuries had given their noblest powers, generations had expended their artistic skill in filling the castle requisitioned for His Excellency, the Commander-in-Chief of the ——th Army, with the choicest treasure. Sun and time had done their best to mellow the dazzle of the accumulated wealth till it shone in subdued grandeur as through a delicate veil. Any man master in that house, who mounted those broad steps and shouted his wishes in those aristocratic rooms, necessarily felt like a king and could not take the war in any other way than as a glorious fairy tale.

Indeed, was there ever a royal household that approached the miraculous more closely? In the kitchen reigned a master of the culinary art, the chef of the best hotel in the country, who in other circumstances would not have been satisfied with double the wages of a general and was now getting only a dollar a day. Yet he was using every bit of his skill. He had never been so eager to please the palate of him whom he served. The roast he prepared was the finest piece of meat to be selected from among the two hundred oxen that daily gave up their lives to the army for the fatherland. The men who served the roast on silver platters, wrought by pupils of Benvenuto for the ancestors of the house, were generals of their trade, who in peace times had had their clothes built in London, and stood about tremblingly awaiting each sign from their master. And this entire retinue, this whole princely household, functioned quite automatically, and —entirely without cost! The master for whom every one slaved never once had to perform that inevitable nuisance of putting his hand in his pocket to draw out his purse. The gasoline circulated inexhaustibly through the veins of the three motor cars, which lounged day and night on the marble flagging of the courtyard. As by magic everything flowed in that eye and palate could desire.

No servant asked for wages, everything seemed to be there of itself, as in fairy castles

where it is enough to wish for a thing in order
to have it.

But that was not all. It was not the whole
of the miracle that the table spread itself every
day of the month and the store-rooms filled
themselves with provisions. When the first of
the month came round, bank-notes instead of
bills came fluttering into the house.

No worry, no disputing, no stinting of one's
self to be borne with a sigh. With an air of
boredom one stuffed his pockets with green-
backs, which were really quite superfluous in
this lazy man's paradise that the war had
opened up to its vassals.

One single lowering cloud now and then
streaked the shining firmament of this won-
derland and cast its shadow on the brow of
His Excellency. Sometimes his pure joy was
disturbed by the thought that the fairy tale
might give way to reality and he might be
awakened from the glorious dream. It was
not peace that His Excellency dreaded. He
never even thought of peace. But what if the

wall so artfully constructed out of human
bodies should begin to totter some day? What
if the enemy were to penetrate all the fortifica-
tions, and discipline were to give way to panic,
and the mighty wall should dissolve into its
component parts, human beings fleeing madly
to save their lives? Then the "Victor of
——," the almighty fairy tale king, would sink
back again into the sordid commonplace of old.
He would have to eke out his existence in some
obscure corner, crowd his trophies into some
modest apartment, and content himself, like
other discharged officers, with being a coffee-
house king. Were he to suffer a single de-
feat, the world would instantly forget its enthusiasm. Another general would assume the
reign, another sovereign would fly through the
town in a motor car, and the vast retinue of
servants would reverently bow before their new
ruler. The old one would be nothing but a
past episode, a scarecrow revealed, which any
sparrow impudently besmirches.

The general's pudgy hand involuntarily

clenched itself, and the dreaded frown, the "storm-signal" that his own soldiers, as well as the enemy, had learned to fear, appeared for a moment on his prominent forehead. Then his face cleared again, and His Excellency looked around proudly.

No! The Victor of —— was not afraid. His wall stood firm and swayed not. For three months every report that emissaries brought to camp had told of the enormous preparations being made by the enemy. For three months they had been storing up ammunition and gathering together their forces for the tremendous offensive. And the offensive had begun the night before. The general knew that the crowd gaily thronging in the sun would not read in the newspaper till the next morning that out at the front a fierce battle had been raging for the past twenty hours, and hardly sixty miles from the promenade shells were bursting without cease, and a heavy rain of hot iron was pouring down upon his soldiers. Three infantry attacks had already been reported as repulsed, and now the artillery was hammering with frenzied fury, a prologue to fresh conflicts during the night.

Well, let them come!

With a jerk, His Excellency sat up, and while his fingers beat on the table in tune to the Blue Danube, a tense expression came into his face, as though he could hear the terrific drumfire raging at the front like a hurricane. His preparations had been made: the human reservoir had been filled to overflowing. Two hundred thousand strong young lads of the very right age lay behind the lines ready at the proper moment to be thrown in front of the steam-roller until it caught and stuck in a marsh of blood and bones. Just let them come! The more, the merrier! The Victor of —— was prepared to add another branch to his laurels, and his eyes sparkled like the medals on his breast.

His adjutant got up from the table next to his, approached hesitatingly, and whispered a few words in His Excellency's ear.

The great man shook his head, waving the adjutant off.

"It is an important foreign newspaper, Your Excellency," the adjutant urged; and when his commander still waved him aside, he added significantly: "The gentleman has brought a letter of recommendation from head-quarters, Your Excellency."

At this the general finally gave in, arose with a sigh, and said, half in jest, half in annoyance to the lady beside him:

"A drumfire would be more welcome!" Then he followed his adjutant and shook hands jovially with the bald civilian, who popped up from his seat and bent at the middle like a penknife snapping shut. His Excellency invited him to be seated.

The war correspondent stammered a few words of admiration, and opened his note-book expectantly, a whole string of questions on his lips. But His Excellency did not let him speak. In the course of time he had constructed for occasions like this a speech in which every point was well thought out and which made a simple impression. He delivered it now, speaking with emphasis and pausing occasionally to recall what came next.

To begin with he spoke of his brave soldiers, praising their courage, their contempt of death, their wonderful deeds of valor. Then he expressed regret at the impossibility of rewarding each soldier according to his merits, and—this in a raised voice—invoked the fatherland's eternal gratitude for such loyalty and self-abnegation even unto death. Pointing to the heavy crop of medals on his chest, he explained that the distinctions awarded him were really an honor done to his men. Finally he wove in a few well-chosen remarks complimenting the enemy's fighting ability and cautious leadership, and concluded with an expression of his unshakable confidence in ultimate victory.

The newspaper man listened respectfully and occasionally jotted down a note. The main thing, of course, was to observe the

Great One's appearance, his manner of speech, his gestures, and to sum up his personality in a few striking phrases.

His Excellency now discarded his military rôle, and changed himself from the Victor of —— into the man of the world.

"You are going to the front now?" he asked with a courteous smile, and responded to the correspondent's enthusiastic "Yes" with a deep, melancholy sigh.

"How fortunate you are! I envy you. You see, the tragedy in the life of the general of to-day is that he cannot lead his men personally into the fray. He spends his whole life preparing for war, he is a soldier in body and soul, and yet he knows the excitement of battle only from hearsay."

The correspondent was delighted with this subjective utterance which he had managed to evoke. Now he could show the commander in the sympathetic rôle of one who renounces, one who cannot always do as he would. He bent over his note-book for an instant. When he looked up again he found to his astonishment that His Excellency's face had completely changed. His brow was furrowed, his eyes stared wide-open with an anxiously expectant look in them at something back of the correspondent.

The correspondent turned and saw a pale, emaciated infantry captain making straight toward His Excellency. The man was grinning and he had a peculiar shambling walk. He came closer and closer, and stared with glassy, glaring eyes, and laughed an ugly idiotic laugh. The adjutant started up from his seat frightened. The veins on His Excellency's forehead swelled up like ropes. The correspondent saw an assassination coming and turned pale. The uncanny captain swayed to within a foot or two of the general and his adjutant, then stood still, giggled foolishly, and snatched at the orders on His Excellency's chest like a child snatching at a beam of light.

"Beautiful—shines beautifully—" he gurgled in a thick voice. Then he pointed his frightfully thin, trembling forefinger up at the sun and shrieked, "Sun!" Next he snatched at the medals again and said, "Shines beautifully." And all the while his restless glance wandered hither and thither as if looking for something, and his ugly, bestial laugh repeated itself after each word.

His Excellency's right fist was up in the air ready for a blow at the fellow's chest for approaching him so disrespectfully, but, instead, he laid his hand soothingly on the poor idiot's shoulder.

"I suppose you have come from the hospital to listen to the music, Captain?" he said, winking to his adjutant. "It's a long ride to the hospital in the street-car. Take my automobile. It's quicker."

"Auto—quicker," echoed the lunatic with his hideous laugh. He patiently let himself be taken by the arm and led away. He turned round once with a grin at the glittering medals, but the adjutant pulled him along.

The general followed them with his eyes until they entered the machine. The "storm-signal" was hoisted ominously between his eyebrows. He was boiling with rage at such carelessness in allowing a creature like that to walk abroad freely. But in the nick of time he remembered the civilian at his side, and controlled himself, and said with a shrug of the shoulders:

"Yes, these are some of the sad aspects of the war. You see, it is just because of such things that the leader must stay behind, where nothing appeals to his heart. No general could ever summon the necessary severity to direct a war if he had to witness all the misery at the front."

"Very interesting," the correspondent breathed gratefully, and closed his book. "I fear I have already taken up too much of Your Excellency's valuable time, but may I be permitted one more question? When does Your Excellency hope for peace?"

The general started, bit his underlip, and

glanced aside with a look that would have made
every staff officer of the ——th Army shake in
his boots.   With a visible effort he put on his
polite smile and pointed across the square to
the open portals of the old cathedral.

"The only advice I can give is for you to go
over there and ask our Heavenly Father.   He
is the only one who can answer that question."

A friendly nod, a hearty handshake, then
His Excellency strode to his office across the
square amid the respectful salutations of the
crowd.

When he entered the building the dreaded
furrow cleaving his brow was deeper than ever.
An orderly tremblingly conducted him to the
office of the head army physician.   For several minutes the entire house held its breath
while the voice of the Mighty One thundered
through the corridors.   He ordered the fine old
physician to come to his table as if he were his
secretary, and dictated a decree forbidding all
the inmates of the hospitals, without distinc-

tion or exception, whether sick or wounded, to leave the hospital premises. "For"—the decree concluded—"if a man is ill, he belongs in bed, and if he feels strong enough to go to town and sit in the coffee-house, he should report at the front, where his duty calls him."

This pacing to and fro with clinking spurs and this thundering at the cowering old doctor calmed his anger. The storm had about blown over when unfortunately the general's notice was drawn to the report from the brigade that was being most heavily beset by the enemy and had suffered desperate losses and was holding its post only in order to make the enterprise as costly as possible to the advancing enemy. Behind it the mines had already been laid, and a whole new division was already in wait in subterranean hiding ready to prepare a little surprise for the enemy after the doomed brigade had gone to its destruction. Of course, the general had not considered it necessary to inform the brigadier that he was holding a lost post and all he was to do was to sell his hide as dearly as possible. The longer the struggle raged the better! And men fight so much more stubbornly if they hope for relief until the very last moment.

All this His Excellency himself had ordained, and he was really greatly rejoiced that the brigade was still holding out after three overwhelming infantry charges. But now a report lay before him which went against all military tradition; and it brought back the storm that had been about to subside.

The major-general (His Excellency made careful note of his name) described the frightful effect of the drumfire in a nervous, talkative way that was most unmilitary. Instead of confining himself to a statement of numbers, he explained at length how his brigade had been decimated and his men's power of resistance was gone. He concluded his report by begging for reinforcements, else it would be impossible for the remnant of his company to withstand the attack to take place that night.

"Impossible? Impossible?" His Excellency blared like a trumpet into the ears of the gentlemen standing motionless around him. "Impossible? Since when is the commander instructed by his subordinates as to what is possible and what is not?"

Blue in the face with rage he took a pen and wrote this single sentence in answer to the report: "The sector is to be held." Underneath he signed his name in the perpendicular scrawl that every school child knew from the picture card of the "Victor of ———." He himself put the envelope into the motor-cyclist's hand for it to be taken to the wireless station, as the telephone wires of the brigade had long since been shot into the ground. Then he blustered like a storm cloud from room to room, stayed half an hour in the card room, had a short interview with the chief of the staff, and asked to have the evening reports sent to the castle. When his rumbling "Good night, gentlemen!" at last resounded in the large hall under the dome, every one heaved a sigh of relief. The guard stood at attention, the chauffeur started the motor, and the big machine plunged into the street with a bellow like a wild beast's. Panting and tooting, it darted its way through the narrow streets out into the open, where the castle like a fairy palace looked down into the misty valley below with its pearly rows of illuminated windows.

With his coat collar turned up, His Excellency sat in the car and reflected as he usually did at this time on the things that had happened during the day. The correspondent came to his mind and the man's stupid question, "When does Your Excellency hope for peace?" Hope? Was it credible that a man who must have some standing in his profession, else he never would have received a letter of recommendation from headquarters, had so little suspicion of how contrary that was to every soldierly feeling? Hope for peace? What good was a general to expect from peace? Could this civilian not comprehend that a commanding general really commanded, was really a general, just in times of war, while in times of peace he was like a strict teacher in galloons, an old duffer who occasionally shouted himself hoarse out of pure ennui? Was he to long for that dreary treadmill existence again? Was he to hope for the time—to please the gentlemen civilians—when he, the victorious leader of the ———th Army, would be used again merely for reviews? Was he to await impatiently going back to that other hopeless struggle between a meager salary and a life polished for show, a struggle in which the lack of money always came out triumphant?

The general leaned back on the cushioned seat in annoyance.

Suddenly the car stopped with a jerk right in the middle of the road. The general started up in surprise and was about to question the chauffeur, when the first big drops of rain fell on his helmet. It was the same storm that earlier in the afternoon had given the men at the front a short respite.

The two corporals jumped out and quickly put up the top. His Excellency sat stark upright, leaned his ear to the wind, and listened attentively. Mingled with the rushing sound of the wind he caught quite clearly, but very —very faintly a dull growling, a hollow, scarcely audible pounding, like the distant echo of trees being chopped down in the woods.

Drumfire!

His Excellency's eyes brightened. A gleam of inner satisfaction passed over his face so recently clouded with vexation.

Thank God! There still was war!

MY COMRADE

IV

MY COMRADE

(A Diary)

THIS world war has given me a comrade, too. You couldn't find a better one.

It is exactly fourteen months ago that I met him for the first time in a small piece of woods near the road to Goerz. Since then he has never left my side for a single moment. We sat up together hundreds of nights through, and still he walks beside me steadfastly.

Not that he intrudes himself upon me. On the contrary. He conscientiously keeps the distance that separates him, the common soldier, from the officer that he must respect in me. Strictly according to regulations he stands three paces off in some corner or be-

hind some column and only dares to cast his
shy glances at me.

He simply wants to be near me. That's all
he asks for, just for me to let him be in my
presence.

Sometimes I close my eyes to be by myself
again, quite by myself for a few moments, as
I used to be before the war. Then he fixes his
gaze upon me so firmly and penetratingly and
with such obstinate, reproachful insistence that
it burns into my back, settles under my eyelids, and so steeps my being with the picture
of him that I look round, if a little time has
passed without his reminding me of his presence.

He has gnawed his way into me, he has
taken up his abode within me. He sits inside
of me like the mysterious magician at moving-
picture shows who turns the crank inside of the
black booth above the heads of the spectators.
He casts his picture through my eyes upon
every wall, every curtain, every flat surface
that my eyes fall on.

But even when there is no background for his picture, even when I frantically look out of the window and stare into the distance so as to be rid of him for a short while, even then he is there, hovering in front of me as though impaled upon the lance of my gaze, like a banner swaying at the head of a parade. If X-rays could penetrate the skull, one would find his picture woven into my brain in vague outline, like the figures in old tapestries.

I remember a trip I took before the war from Munich to Vienna on the Oriental Express. I looked out upon the autumnal mellowness of the country around the Bavarian lakes and the golden glow of the Wiener Wald. But across all this glory that I drank in leaning back on the comfortable seat in luxurious contentment, there steadily ran an ugly black spot—a flaw in the window-pane. That is the way my obstinate comrade flits across woods and walls, stands still when I stand still, dances over the faces of passers-by, over the asphalt paving wet from the rain, over everything my eyes happen to fall upon.   He interposes himself between me and the world, just like that flaw in the window-pane, which degraded everything I saw to the quality of the background that it made.

The physicians, of course, know better. They do not believe that He lives in me and stays by me like a sworn comrade.   From the standpoint of science it rests with me not to drag him round any longer, but to give him his dismissal, precisely as I might have freed myself from the annoying spot by angrily smashing the window-pane.   The physicians do not believe that one human being can unite himself at death with another human being and continue to live on in him with obstinate persistence.   It is their opinion that a man standing at a window should see the house opposite but never the wall of the room behind his back.

The physicians only believe in things that *are*. Such superstitions as that a man can carry dead men within him and see them stand-

ing in front of him so distinctly that they hide
a picture behind them from his sight, do not
come within the range of the gentlemen's rea-
soning.   In their lives death plays no part.
A patient who dies ceases to be a patient.
And what does the day know of the night,
though the one forever succeeds the other?

But I know it is not I who forcibly drag
the dead comrade through my life.   I know
that the dead man's life within me is stronger
than my own life.   It may be that the shapes
I see flitting across the wall papers, cowering
in corners and staring into the lighted room
from dark balconies, and knocking so hard on
the windows that the panes rattle, are only
visions and nothing more.   Where do they
come from?   *My* brain furnishes the picture,
my eyes provide the projection, but it is the
dead man that sits at the crank.   He tends to
the film.   The show begins when it suits Him
and does not stop as long as He turns the
crank.   How can I help seeing what He
shows me?   If I close my eyes the picture

falls upon the inside of my lids, and the drama plays inside of me instead of dancing far away over doors and walls.

I should be the stronger of the two, they say. But you cannot kill a dead man, the physicians should know that.

Are not the paintings by Titian and Michael Angelo still hanging in the museums centuries after Titian and Michael Angelo lived? And the pictures that a dying man chiseled into my brain fourteen months ago with the prodigious strength of his final agony—are they supposed to disappear simply because the man that created them is lying in his soldier's grave?

Who, when he reads or hears the word "woods," does not see some woods he has once walked through or looked out on from a train window? Or when a man speaks of his dead father does he not see the face that has long been rotting in the grave appear again, now stern, now gentle, now in the rigidity of the last moments? What would our whole exist-ence be without these visions which, each at its

own word, rise up for moments out of oblivion
as if in the glare of a flashlight?

Sick? Of course. The world is sore, and
will have no words or pictures that do not have
reference to the wholesale graves. Not for a
moment can the comrade within me join the
rest of the dead, because everything that hap-
pens is as a flashlight falling upon him.
There's the newspaper each morning to begin
with: "Ships sunk," "Attacks repulsed."
And immediately the film reels off a whirl of
gasping, struggling men, fingers rising out of
mountainous waves grasping for life once more,
faces disfigured by pain and fury. Every conversation that one overhears, every shop window, every breath that is drawn is a reminder
of the wholesale carnage. Even the silence of
the night is a reminder. Does not each tick
of the second-hand mark the death rattle of
thousands of men? In order to hear the hell
raging yonder on the other side of the thick
wall of air, is it not enough to know of chins

blown off, throats cut open, and corpses locked in a death embrace?

If a man were lying comfortably in bed and then found out for certain that some one next door was being murdered, would you say he was sick if he jumped up out of bed with his heart pounding? And are we anything but next door to the places where thousands duck down in frantic terror, where the earth spits mangled fragments of bodies up into the sky, and the sky hammers down on the earth with fists of iron? Can a man live at a distance from his crucified self when the whole world resounds with reminders of these horrors?

No!

It is the others that are sick. They are sick who gloat over news of victories and see conquered miles of territory rise resplendent above mounds of corpses. They are sick who stretch a wall of flags between themselves and their humanity so as not to know what crimes are being committed against their brothers in the beyond that they call "the front." Every man

is sick who still can think, talk, discuss, sleep,
knowing that other men holding their own entrails in their hands are crawling like half-
crushed worms across the furrows in the fields
and before they reach the stations for the
wounded are dying off like animals, while
somewhere, far away, a woman with passionate
longing is dreaming beside an empty bed. All
those are sick who can fail to hear the moaning,
the gnashing of teeth, the howling, the crashing and bursting, the wailing and cursing and
agonizing in death, because the murmur of
everyday affairs is around them or the blissful
silence of night.

It is the deaf and the blind that are sick,
not I!

It is the dull ones that are sick, those whose
souls sing neither compassion for others nor
their own anger. All those numerous people
are sick who, like a violin without strings,
merely echo every sound. Or would you say
that the man whose memory is like a photo-
graphic plate on which the light has fallen and

which cannot record any more impressions, is the healthy man? Is not memory the very highest possession of every human being? It is the treasure that animals do not own, because they are incapable of holding the past and reviving it.

Am I to be cured of my memory as from an illness? Why, without my memory I would not be myself, because every man is built up of his memories and really lives only as long as he goes through life like a loaded camera. Supposing I could not tell where I lived in my childhood, what color my father's eyes and my mother's hair were, and supposing at any moment that I were called upon to give an account, I could not turn the leaves of the past and point to the right picture, how quick they would be to diagnose my case as feeblemindedness, or imbecility. Then, to be considered mentally normal, must one treat one's brain like a slate to be sponged off and be able at command to tear out pictures that have burned the most hideous misery into the soul, and throw them away as one does leaves from an album of photographs?

One man died before my eyes, he died hard, torn asunder after a frightful struggle between the two Titans, Life and Death. Am I sick, then, if I experience all over again all the phases of his agonizing—preserved in my brain like snapshots—as long as every happening inexorably opens the pages of this series? And the other people, are they well, those, I mean, who skip the pages as though they were blank that record the dismemberment, the mutilation, the crushing of their brothers, the slow writhing to death of men caught in barbed wire entanglements?

Tell me, my dear doctors, at just what point am I to begin to forget?

Am I to forget I was in the war? Am I to forget the moment in the smoky railway station when I leaned out of the car window and saw my boy ashen white, with compressed lips, standing beside his mother, and I made a poor show of cheerfulness and talked of seeing

them soon again, while my eyes greedily
searched the features of my wife and child, and
my soul drank in the picture of them like
parched lips after a many days' march drink-
ing in the water so madly longed for? Am I
to forget the choking and the bitterness in my
mouth when the train began to move and the
distance swallowed up my child, my wife, my
world?

And the whole ride to death, when I was
the only military traveler in a car full of
happy family men off for a summer Sunday
in the country—am I to tear it out of my
memory like so much cumbersome waste paper? Am I to forget how I felt when it grew
quieter at each station, as though life were
crumbling away, bit by bit, until at midnight
only one or two sleepy soldiers remained in my
coach and an ashen young face drawn with
sorrow hovered about the flickering lamplight? Must one actually be sick if it is like
an incurable wound always to feel that leavetaking of home and warmth, that riding away

with hatred and danger awaiting one at the
end of the trip? Is there anything harder to
understand—when have men done anything
madder—than this: to race through the night
at sixty miles an hour, to run away from all
love, all security, to leave the train and take another train because it is the only one that goes
to where invisible machines belch red-hot pieces
of iron and Death casts out a finely meshed net
of steel and lead to capture men? Who will
obliterate from my soul the picture of that
small dirty junction, the shivering, sleepy soldiers without any intoxication or music in their
blood, looking wistfully after the civilian's
train and its brightly lighted windows as it disappeared behind the trees with a jolly blow of
its whistle? Who will obliterate the picture of
that exchanging for Death in the drab light of
early dawn?

And supposing I could cross out that first
endless night as something settled and done
with, would not the next morning remain,
when our train stopped at a switch in the mid-

dle of a wide, dewy meadow, and we were told that we had to wait to let hospital trains go by? How shall I ever banish the memory of those thick exhalations of lysol and blood blown upon the happy fields from a dragon's nostrils? Won't I forever see those endless serpents creeping up so indolently, as though surfeited with mangled human flesh? From hundreds of windows white bandages gleamed and dull, glassy eyes stared out. Lying, crouching, on top of each other, body to body, they even hung on to the running-boards like bloody bunches of grapes, an overflowing abundance of distress and agony. And those wretched remains of strength and youth, those bruised and battered men, looked with pity, yes, *with pity,* at our train. Am I really sick because those glances of warm compassion from bleeding cripples to sound, strapping young fellows burn in my soul with a fire never to be extinguished? An apprehension sent a chill through our whole train, the foreboding of a hell that one would rather run away from

wrapped in bloody bandages than go to meet
whole and strong. And when this shudder
of apprehension has turned into reality, into
experience and memory, is it to be shaken off
as long as such trains still meet every day? A
casual remark about the transfer of troops,
news of fresh battles inevitably recall this first
actual contact with the war, just as a certain
note when struck will produce a certain tone,
and I see the tracks and ties and stones spat-
tered with blood, shining in the early morning
light of a summer day—signposts pointing to
the front.

"The Front!"

Am *I* really the sick person because I cannot
utter that word or write it down without
my tongue growing coated from the intense
hatred I feel? Are not the others mad who
look upon this wholesale cripple-and-corpse-
factory with a mixture of religious devotion,
romantic longing and shy sympathy? Would
it not be wiser once for a change to examine
those others for the state of their mind? Must

I disclose it to my wise physicians, who watch over me so compassionately, that all this mischief is the work of a few words that have been let loose upon humanity like a pack of mad dogs?

Front—Enemy—Hero's death—Victory—the curs rage through the world with frothing mouth and rolling eyes. Millions who have been carefully inoculated against smallpox, cholera and typhoid fever are chased into madness. Millions, on either side, are packed into cars—ride, singing, to meet each other at the front—hack, stab, shoot at each other, blow each other into bits, give their flesh and their bones for the bloody hash out of which the dish of peace is to be cooked for those fortunate ones who give the flesh of their calves and oxen to their fatherland for a hundred per cent profit, instead of carrying their own flesh to market for fifty cents a day.

Suppose the word "war" had never been invented and had never been hallowed through the ages and decked with gay trappings. Who would dare to supplement the deficient phrase, "declaration of war," by the following speech?

"After long, fruitless negotiations our emissary to the government of X left to-day. From the window of his parlor car he raised his silk hat to the gentlemen who had escorted him to the station, and he will not meet them with a friendly smile again until *you* have made corpses of many hundreds of thousands of men in the country of X. Up then! Squeeze yourself into box-cars meant for six horses or twenty-eight men! Ride to meet them, those other men. Knock them dead, hack off their heads, live like wild beasts in damp excavations, in neglect, in filth, overrun with lice, until we shall deem the time has come again for our emissary to take a seat in a parlor car and lift his silk hat, and in ornate rooms politely and aristocratically dispute over the advantages which our big merchants and manufacturers are to derive from the slaughter. Then as many of you as are not rotting under the ground or hobbling on crutches and begging from door to door may return to your half-starved families, and may—nay must!—take up your work again with redoubled energy, more indefatigably and yet with fewer demands than before, so as to be able to pay in sweat and privation for the shoes that you wore out in hundreds of marches and the clothes that decayed on your bodies."

A fool he who would sue for a following in such terms! But *no* fools they who are the victims, who freeze, starve, kill, and let themselves be killed, just because they have learned to believe that this must be so, once the mad dog War has burst his chains and bitten the world.

Is this what the wars were like from which the word "war" has come down to us? Did not war use to guarantee booty? Were not the mercenaries led on by hopes of a gay, lawless life—women and ducats and gold-caparisoned steeds? Is this cowering under iron discipline, this holding out of your head to be chopped off, this passive play with monsters that spill their hellish cauldron on you from out

of the blue distance still "war"? War was the
collision of the superfluous forces, the ruffians
of all nations. Youth, for whom the town had
grown too small and the doublet too tight, ven-
tured out, intoxicated by the play of its own
muscles. And now shall the same word hold
good when men already anchored to house and
home are torn away and whipped into the ranks
and laid out before the enemy, and made to
wait, defenseless, in dull resignation, like
supers in this duel of the munition industries?

Is it right to misuse the word "war" as a
standard when it is not courage and strength
that count, but explosive bombs and the length
of range of the guns and the speed with which
women and children turn out shells? We
used to speak with horror of the tyrants
of dark ages, who threw helpless men and
women to the lions and tigers; but now is there
one of us who would not mention them with
respect in comparison with the rulers who are
at present directing the struggle between men
and machines, as though it were a puppet show
at the end of telegraph wires, and who are

animated by the delightful hope that our supply of human flesh may outlast the enemy's
supply of steel and iron?

No! All words coined before this carnage
began are too beautiful and too honest, like
the word "front," which I have learned to
abhor. Are you "facing" the enemy when
their artillery is hidden behind mountains and
sends death over a distance of a day's journey,
and when their sappers come creeping up
thirty feet below the surface? And your
"front" is a terminal station, a little house all
shot up, behind which the tracks have been
torn up because the trains turn back here after
unloading their cargo of fresh, sunburned men,
to call for them again when they have emerged
from the machines with torn limbs and faces
covered with verdigris.

It was towards evening when I got off the
train at this terminal. A bearded soldier with
his right arm in a sling was sitting on the
ground leaning against the iron railing around
the platform. When he saw me pass by, quite

spick and span, he stroked his right arm tenderly with his left hand and threw me an ugly look of hatred and called out through clenched teeth:

"Yes, Lieutenant, here's the place for man salad."

Am I to forget the wicked grin that widened his mouth, already distorted by pain? Am I sick because each time I hear the word "front" an echo, "man salad," inevitably croaks in my ears? Or are the others sick who do not hear "man salad," but swallow down the cowardly stuff written by our war bards, who try like industrious salesmen to make the brand "world war" famous, because in reward they will have the privilege of dashing about in automobiles like commanding generals instead of being forced to face death in muddy ditches and be bossed by a little corporal?

Are there really human beings of flesh and blood who can still take a newspaper in their hands and not foam at the mouth with rage? Can one carry in one's brain the picture of

wounded men lying exposed on slimy fields in
the pouring rain, slowly, dumbly bleeding to
death, and yet quietly read the vile stuff written about "perfect hospital service," "smoothly
running ambulances," and "elegantly papered
trenches," with which these fellows poetize
themselves free from military service?

Men come home with motionless, astonished
eyes, still reflecting death. They walk about
shyly, like somnambulists in brightly lighted
streets. In their ears there still resound the
bestial howls of fury that they themselves bellowed into the hurricane of the drumfire so as
to keep from bursting from inner stress. They
come loaded down, like beasts of burden, with
horrors, the astonished looks of bayoneted,
dying foes on their conscience—and they don't
dare open their mouths because everybody, wife
and child included, grinds out the same tune,
a flow of curious questions about shells, gas
bombs and bayonet attacks. So the days of the
furlough expire, one by one, and the return
to death is almost a deliverance from the shame

of being a coward in disguise among the friends
at home, to whom dying and killing have become mere commonplaces.

So be it, my dear doctors! It is an honor to
be charged with madness if those villains are
not called mad who, to save their own necks,
have so gloriously hardened the people's hearts
and abolished pity and implanted pride in the
enemy's suffering, instead of acting as the one
intermediary between distress and power and
arousing the conscience of the world by going
to the most frequented places and shouting
"Man Sal-ad" through a megaphone so loud
and so long that at length all those whose
fathers, husbands, brothers, sons, have gone
to the corpse-factory will be seized with terror
and all the throats in the world will be *one* echo
to "Man Sal-ad!"

If you were here right now, dear doctors, I
could show you my comrade, summoned to this
room in the very body by the flames of hate
against news from the front and against the
indifference of the hinterland. I feel him

standing behind my back, but his face is lying on the white sheet in front of me, like a faint water-mark, and my pen races frantically so as to cover his eyes at least with letters and hide their reproachful stare.

Large, widening, hideously distorted, his face, slowly swelling, rises from the paper like the face of Jesus of the handkerchief.

It was just like this that the three war correspondents saw him lying at the edge of the woods on that midsummer morning and—turned away involuntarily with almost the military exactness of soldiers at a "right about face." Their visit was meant for *me!* I was to furnish them with carriage and horses because the automobile that was to have darted them through the danger zone was lying on the road to Goerz with a broken axle.

Charming gentlemen, in wonderfully well-cut breeches and traveling caps, looking as if they had stepped out of a Sherlock Holmes motion picture. They offered to carry letters back and deliver messages, and they found

everything on my place perfectly fascinating,
and laughed heartily at my mattress of willow
twigs—and were particularly grateful when
the carriage stood ready to carry them off before the daily bombardment of the Italians
began.

On driving out of the woods they had to
pass the wounded man again with the hideously
disfigured face. He was crouching on the
meadow. But this time they did not see him.
As if at command they turned their heads the
other way and with animated gestures viewed
the damage done by an air raid the day before,
as though they were already sitting over a table
in a coffee-house.

I lost my breath, as though I had run a long
distance up-hill. The place where I stood suddenly seemed strange and altered. Was that
the same piece of woods into which shells had
so often come crashing, which the huge Cap-
roni planes had circled about with wide-spread
wings like vultures, shedding bombs, while our
machine guns lashed the leaves with a hail-

storm of shot? Was it out of *this* piece of woods that three men had just driven off, healthy, unscathed, gaily waving their caps? Where was the wall that held us others imprisoned under the cracking branches? Was there not a door that opened only to let out pale, sunken cheeks, feverish eyes, or mangled limbs?

The carriage rolled lightly over the field, trampled down brown, and the one thing missing to make it the perfect picture of a pleasure trip was the brilliant red of a Baedeker.

Those men were riding back home.

To wife and child, perhaps?

A painful pulling and tugging, as though my eyes were caught to the carriage wheels. Then my body rebounded—as if torn off—back into emptiness, and—at that moment, just when my soul was as if ploughed up by the carriage and laid bare and defenseless by yearning—at that moment the experience sprang upon me—with one dreadful leap, one single bite—incurable for the rest of my life.

Unsuspecting, I crossed over to the wounded man upon whom the three had so unceremoniously turned their backs, as though he did not also belong to the interesting museum of shell holes that they had come to inspect. He was cowering near the dirty ragged little Red Cross flag, with his head between his knees, and did not hear me come up. Behind him lay the brown spot which stood out from the green still left on the field like a circus ring. The wounded soldiers who gathered here every morning at dawn to be driven to the field hospital in the wagons that brought us ammunition had rubbed this spot in like a favorite corner of a sofa.

How many I had seen crouching there like that, for ten—often twelve hours, when the wagons had left too early, or had been overcrowded, or, after violent fighting, had stood waiting in line at the munitions depot behind the lines. Happy fellows, some of them, with broken arms or legs, the war slang, "a thousand-dollar shot," on their pale, yet laughing lips—enviously ogled by the men with slight wounds or the men sick with typhoid fever, who would all gladly have sacrificed a thousand dollars and a limb into the bargain for the same certainty of not having to return to the front again.   How many I had seen rolling on the ground, biting into the earth in their agony— how many in the pouring rain, half buried already in the mud, their bodies ripped open, groaning and whimpering and outbellowing the storm.

This man seemed to be only slightly hurt in the right leg.   The blood had oozed out on one spot through the hastily made bandage, so I offered him my first-aid package, besides cognac and cigarettes.   But he did not move. It was not until I laid my hand on his shoulder that he raised his head—and the face he showed me threw me back like a blow on the chest.

His mouth and nose had come apart, and crept like a thick vine up his right cheek— which was no longer a cheek.   A chunk of bluish red flesh swelled up there, covered by skin stretched to bursting and shining from being drawn so tight. The whole right side of his face seemed more like an exotic fruit than a human countenance, while from the left side, from out of grey twitching misery, a sad, frightened eye looked up at me.

Violent terror slung itself round my neck like a lasso.

What was it? Such a frightful thing as that even this field, this waiting-room to the Beyond, had never witnessed before. Even the awful recollection of another wounded man who had stood at this same spot a few days before, his hands looking as though they were modeling something, while in actuality they were carefully holding his own entrails—even that hideous recollection faded before the sight of this Janus head, all peace, all gentle humanity on one side; all war, all distorted, puffed-up image of fiendish hatred on the other side.

"Shrapnel?" I stammered timidly.

The answer was confused. All I could get

out of it was that a dumdum bullet had smashed his right shinbone.   But what was that he kept mumbling about a hook each time his hand trembled up to his glowing cheek?

I could not understand him; for the thing he had gone through still seethed in his veins so violently that he spoke as though it were just then happening and I were witnessing it. His peasant's mind could not comprehend that there were people who had not seen or heard of the tremendous misery of the last hours he had gone through.   So it was more by guess-work that I gradually pieced together his story from unfinished sentences, coarse oaths, and groans.

For a whole night, after a repulsed attack on the enemy's trench, he had lain with a broken leg, unconscious, near our own wire entanglements. At dawn they threw out the iron grappling hook for him, with which they pull over into the trench the corpses of friend and foe so as to be able to bury them uncere-moniously before the sun of Goerz has a chance

to do its work. With this hook, dipped in
hundreds of corpses, a dunce—"God damn
him!"—had torn his cheek open before a more
skilful hand caught hold of it and got him
over safely. And now he asked humbly to be
taken away to the hospital quickly, because
he was worried—about his leg and being a crippled beggar the rest of his life.

I ran off as though mad dogs were at my
heels, over rocks and roots, through the woods
to the next detachment. In vain! In the
whole woods there was not a single vehicle to
be found. I had given up the last one to those
three war correspondents.

Why had I not asked them to take the one
wounded man lying on the field along with
them and leave him at the hospital that they
would pass? Why had they themselves not
thought of doing their human duty? Why?

I clenched my fists in impotent fury and
caught myself reaching for my revolver as
though I could still shoot those gay sparks in
their carriage.

Breathless, overheated from the long race, I tottered back, my knees trembling the whole way. I felt utterly broken, as though I were carrying on my shoulders a picture, weighing a ton, of men who for sport angle for human carrion.

An odd choking and tickling came into my throat—a sensation I had not known since childhood—when, back at my post again, I had to listen to the low whimpering of the help-less man.

He was no longer alone. In my absence a little band of slightly wounded men had joined him. Peering between the tree trunks I saw them sitting in a circle on the field, while the man who had been hooked was hopping about holding on to his injured leg and tossing his head from one shoulder to the other.

Towards noon I sent my corporals in search of a vehicle, promising them a princely reward, while I ran to the field again with my whisky flask.

He was no longer dancing about. He was

kneeling in the center of the circle of wounded men, his body bent over, rolling his head on the ground as though it were a thing apart from himself. Suddenly he jumped up with such a yell of fury that a frightened murmur came even from the line of wounded men, who had been sitting there indifferent, sunk in their own suffering.

That was no longer anything human. The man's skin could not stand any more stretching and had burst. The broad splits ran apart like the lines of a compass and in the middle the raw flesh glowed and gushed out.

And he yelled! He hammered with his fist on the enormous purplish lump, until he fell to his knees again moaning under the blows of his own hand.

It was dark already when—at last!—they came and carted him away. And when the night slowly wove its web of mist in the woods and I lay wrapped in a mound of blankets, the only one who was still awake in the throng of black tree-trunks that moved closer together in the darkness—there he was back again, standing up stiff in the moonlight, his tortured cheek, huge as a pumpkin, shining blue against the black shadows of the trees. It glimmered like a will-o'-the-wisp, now here, now there. Night after night. It shone into every dream, so that I forced my eyelids open with my fingers—until, after ten frightful nights, my body broke down and was carried, a shrieking, convulsed heap, to the same hospital in which He had succumbed to blood-poisoning.

And now I am a madman! You can read it, black on white, on the placard at the head of my bed. They pat me on the back soothingly, like a shying horse, when I flare up and ask to be let out of this place in which *the others* should be shut up.

But the others are free! From my window I can look over the garden wall into the street, and see them hurrying along, raising their hats, shaking hands, and crowding in front of the latest bulletin. I see women and girls, dressed coquettishly, tripping along with pride shining in their eyes, beside men whom a cross on the breast brands as murderers. I see widows in long black veils—still patient. I see lads with flowers stuck in their helmets ready to leave for the war. And not one of them rebels! Not one of them sees bruised, mangled men cowering in dark corners, men ripped apart by grappling hooks, men with their entrails gushing out, and men with blue shining cheeks.

They go by under my window, gesticulating, enthusiastic; because the enthusiastic phrases arrive coined fresh every day from the mint, and each person feels sheltered and enveloped in a warmth of assent if the phrases ring clear from his lips. I know that they keep quiet even when they would like to speak, to cry out, to scream. I know that they hunt down "slackers," and have no word of abuse for those who are a thousand times worse cowards, those who clearly recognise the utter senselessness of this butchery of millions, yet will not open their mouths for fear of the censure of the thoughtless crowd.

From my window I can see the whole globe spinning round like a crazy whirligig, whipped on by haughty lords in cunning calculation and by venal servants in sneaking submissiveness.

I see the whole pack! The bawlers who are too empty and too lazy to develop their own selves and want to puff themselves with the glittering praise meant for their herd. The scoundrels who are protected by the masses, carried by them and fed by them, and who look up sanctimoniously to a bogy of their own invention, and hammer that bogy into the conscience of millions of good men, until the mass has been forged that has neither heart nor brain, but only fury and blind faith. I see the whole game proceeding madly in blood and agony. I see the spectators going by indifferently, and I am called a madman when I raise the window to call down to them that the sons they have born and bred, the men they have loved are being chased like wild animals, are being butchered like cattle.

Those fools down there, who for the sake of respectable condolence calls, for a neighbor's eyes raised heavenward in sympathy, sacrificed the splendor and warmth of their lives, who threw their flesh and blood into the barbed wire entanglements, to rot as carrion on the fields or be hooked in with grappling hooks, who have no other consolation than that the "enemy" have had the same done to them— those fools remain free; and in their despicable vanity and wicked patience they may daily shove fresh hecatombs out to the cannons. But I must stay here impotent—left alone with the relentless comrade that my conscience gives birth to over again every day.

I stand at my window and between me and the street lie piled high the bodies of the many I saw bleeding. And I stand here powerless —because the revolver that was given me to shoot down poor homesick devils, forced into a uniform by iron necessity, has been taken from me, out of fear that I might dislodge a few mass murderers from their security and send them as a warning example down to their victims.

So I must stay here, as a seer over the blind —behind iron gratings. And all I can do is consign these leaves to the wind—every day write it all down again and keep scattering the pages out on the street.

I will write indefatigably. I will sow the whole world with my pages. Until the seed shall sprout in every heart, until every bedroom will be entered by a blue apparition—a dear dead one showing his wounds; and at last, at last, the glorious song of the world's redemption will resound under my window, the wrathful cry shouted by a million throats:

"Man Sal-ad!"

A HERO'S DEATH

V

A HERO'S DEATH

THE staff physician had not understood. He shook his head, vexed, and looked questioningly over the rims of his glasses at his assistant.

But his assistant had not understood either, and was embarrassed, and stood stiffly without saying anything.

The only one who seemed to have any clue at all to the man's ravings was his orderly. For two tears glistened on the upturned ends of his waxed mustache. But the orderly spoke nothing but Hungarian, and the staff physician turned away with a muttered "blooming idiot." Followed by his flaxen-haired assistant, he made his way toward the operating room, panting and perspiring.

The huge ball of cotton, inside of which, ac-

cording to the placard hanging at the top of
the bed, was hidden the head of First Lieutenant of the Reserves, Otto Kadar, of the
——th Regiment of Field Artillery, sank back
on the pillow, and Miska seated himself again
on his knapsack, snuffed up his tears, put his
head between his big unwashed hands, and
speculated despairingly about his future.

For it was plain that his Lieutenant could
not last much longer. Miska knew what was
hidden in the huge cotton ball. He had seen
the crushed skull and the horrible grey mess
under the bloody splinters which were the
brains of his poor Lieutenant, who had been
such a good man and kind superior. Miska
could not hope for such wonderful luck a
second time. You didn't come across such a
kind-hearted master twice in your life. The
many, many slices of salami that the Lieutenant always had given him from his own store
of provisions, the gentle, cordial words that
Miska had heard him whisper to every
wounded man—all the memories of the long,

bloody months he had gone through dully be-·
side his master almost like a comrade, rose to
his mind. He felt dreadfully sorry for himself, the good fellow did, in his infinite defenselessness against the huge war machine into
which he would now be thrown again without
the sure support of his kind Lieutenant next
to him.

His broad peasant's head between his hands,
he crouched like a dog at the feet of his dying
master, and the tears rolled gently down his
cheeks and stuck one by one on the ends of his
mustache glued with dust and pomade.

It was not quite clear to Miska either just
why the poor Lieutenant kept clamoring so
frightfully for his talking-machine. All he
knew was that the officers had been sitting
under cover, listening to the Rakoczy March
on the phonograph, when suddenly that ac-
cursed shell burst upon them and everything
disappeared in smoke and earth. He himself
had been knocked unconscious by a heavy board
which came out of a clear sky and hit him on

the back. He had fallen flat and it was an eternity before he got his breath back again.

Then—then—Miska's recollections of things after this were a bit hazy—then he remembered an indescribable heap of splintered boards and fallen beams, a hash of rags, cement, earth, human limbs, and quantities of blood. And then—then he remembered—young Meltzar. Meltzar was still sitting upright with his back against the remains of the wall, and the record that had just played the Rakoczy March and had miraculously remained whole was perched on the place where his head belonged. But his head was not there. It was gone—completely gone, while the black record remained, also leaning against the wall, directly on top of the bloodsoaked collar. It was awful. Not one of the soldiers had dared touch the upright body with the record exactly like a head on its neck.

Brrr! A cold shiver ran down Miska's back at the recollection, and his heart stopped beating in fright when just at that moment the Lieutenant again began to scream:

"Phonograph! Only a phonograph!"

Miska jumped up and saw the huge ball of cotton lift itself with an effort from the pillow, and his officer's one remaining eye fix greedily upon some invisible object. He stood there ashamed, as though guilty of a crime, when indignant glances were darted at him from the other beds in the ward.

"This is unbearable!" cried a Major, who had been severely wounded, from the other end of the long ward. "Carry the man out."

But the Major spoke German, and Miska was more than ever at sea. He wiped the sweat of anguish from his brow and explained to a lieutenant in the next bed, since his master could not hear what he said anyhow, that the phonograph had been broken—broken into a thousand pieces, else he would never have left it there, but would surely have brought it along as he had brought everything else belonging to his Lieutenant that he had managed to find.

No one answered him. As at a word of command, each one of the officers the whole length of the ward stuck his head under his pillow and pulled the covers over his ears so as not to hear that horrible gurgling laugh which changed into a howl or into infuriated cries for the phonograph. The old Major even wrapped his blood-stained cloak around his head like a turban.

"Lieutenant! I beg pardon, Lieutenant ——" Miska begged, and very, very gently stroked his master's quivering knees with his big hard palms.

But Lieutenant Kadar heard him not. Neither did he feel the heavy hand resting on his knees. For, opposite him, young Meltzar was still sitting with a flat, black, round head on his neck on which the Rakoczy March was engraved in spirals. And all at once the officer realized that for the past six months he had done poor Meltzar a grievous injustice. How could the poor fellow help his stupidity, how could he help his silly, high-flown patriotic talk? How could he possibly have had sensible ideas with a record for a head? Poor Meltzar!

Lieutenant Kadar simply could not understand why it was that six months before, right away, when young Meltzar announced his entrance into the battery, he had not guessed what they had done to the boy in the hinterland.

They had given him a different head. They had unscrewed the handsome fair young head of a lad of eighteen and in its place put a black, scratched-up disc, which could do nothing but squeak the Rakoczy March. That had now been proved! How the boy must have suffered whenever his superior officer, his senior by twenty years, inflicted long sermons on him about humanity! With the flat, round disc that they had put on him he of course could not comprehend that the Italian soldiers being led past the battery, reeking with blood and in rags, would also much rather have stayed at home, if a bulletin on the street corner had not forced them to leave their homes immediately, just as the mobilization in Hungary had forced the Hungarian gunners to leave their homes.

Now for the first time Lieutenant Kadar comprehended the young man's unbending resistance to him. Now at last he realized why this boy, who could have been his son, had so completely ignored his wisest, kindest admonitions and explanations, and had always responded by whistling the Rakoczy March through clenched teeth and hissing the stereotyped fulmination, "The dogs ought to be shot to pieces."

So then it was not because of his being young and stupid that Meltzar had behaved as he did; not because he had come direct from the military academy to the trenches. The phonograph record was to blame, the phonograph record!

Lieutenant Kadar felt his veins swell up like ropes and his blood pound on his temples like blows on an anvil, so great was his wrath against the wrongdoers who had treacherously unscrewed poor Meltzar's lovely young head from his body.

And—this was the most gruesome—as he now thought of his subordinates and fellow-officers, he saw them all going about exactly like poor Meltzar, without heads on their bodies. He shut his eyes and tried to recall the looks of his gunners—in vain! Not a single face rose before his mind's eye. He had spent months and months among those men and had not discovered until that moment that not one of them had a head on his shoulders. Otherwise he would surely have remembered whether his gunner had a mustache or not and whether the artillery captain was light or dark. No! Nothing stuck in his mind—nothing but phonograph records, hideous, black, round plates lying on bloody blouses.

The whole region of the Isonzo suddenly lay spread out way below him like a huge map such as he had often seen in illustrated papers. The silver ribbon of the river wound in and out

among hills and coppices, and Lieutenant
Kadar soared high above the welter down below without motor or aeroplane, but borne
along merely by his own outspread arms.
And everywhere he looked, on every hill and
in every hollow, he saw the horns of innumerable talking-machines growing out of the
ground. Thousands upon thousands of those
familiar cornucopias of bright lacquer with
gilt edges pointed their open mouths up at
him. And each one was the center of a
swarming ant-hill of busy gunners carrying
shot and shell.

And now Lieutenant Kadar saw it very distinctly: all the men had records on their necks
like young Meltzar. Not a single one carried
his own head. But when the shells burst with
a howl from the lacquered horns and flew
straight into an ant-hill, then the flat, black
discs broke apart and at the very same instant
changed back into real heads. From his height
Lieutenant Kadar saw the brains gush out of
the shattered discs and the evenly-marked sur-

faces turn on the second into ashen, agonized human countenances.

Everything seemed to be revealed now in one stroke to the dying lieutenant—all the secrets of the war, all the problems he had brooded over for many months past. So he had the key to the riddle. These people evidently did not get their heads back until they were about to die. Somewhere—somewhere— far back—far back of the lines, their heads had been unscrewed and replaced by records that could do nothing but play the Rakoczy March. Prepared in this fashion, they had been jammed into the trains and sent to the front, like poor Meltzar, like himself, like all of them.

In a fury of anger, the ball of cotton tossed itself up again with a jerk. Lieutenant Kadar wanted to jump out of bed and reveal the secret to his men, and urge them to insist upon having their heads back again. He wanted to whisper the secret to each individual along the entire front, from Plava all the way down to the sea. He wanted to tell it to each gunner, each soldier in the infantry and even to the Italians over there! He even wanted to tell it to the Italians. The Italians, too, had had records screwed on to their necks. And they should go back home, too, back to Verona, to Venice, to Naples, where their heads lay piled up in the store-houses for safe-keeping until the war was over. Lieutenant Kadar wanted to run from one man to another, so as to help each individual to recover his head, whether friend or foe.

But all at once he noticed he could not walk. And he wasn't soaring any more either. Heavy iron weights clamped his feet down to the bed to keep him from revealing the great secret.

Well, then, he would shout it out in a roar, in a voice supernaturally loud that would sound above the bursting of the shells and the blare of trumpets on the Day of Judgment, and proclaim the truth from Plava to Trieste,

even into the Tyrol. He would shout as no
man had ever shouted before:

"Phonograph!—Bring the heads!—Phonograph!——"

Here his voice suddenly broke with a gurgling sound of agony right in the midst of his
message of salvation. It hurt too much. He
could not shout. He felt as though at each
word a sharp needle went deep into his brain.

A needle?

Of course! How could he have forgotten
it? His head had been screwed off, too. He
wore a record on his neck, too, like all the
others. When he tried to say something, the
needle stuck itself into his skull and ran mercilessly along all the coils of his brain.

No! He could not bear it! He'd rather
keep quiet—keep the secret to himself. Only
not to feel that pain—that maddening pain in
his head!

But the machine ran on. Lieutenant Kadar
grabbed his head with both hands and dug his
nails deep into his temples. If he didn't stop

that thing in time from going round and round, then his revolving head would certainly break his neck in a few seconds.

Icy drops of anguish flowed from all his pores.

"Miska!" he yelled in the extreme of his distress.

But Miska did not know what to do.

The record kept on revolving and joyously thrummed the Rakoczy March. All the sinews in the Lieutenant's body grew tense. Again and again he felt his head slip from between his hands—his spine was already rising before his eyes! With a last, frantic effort he tried once more to get his hands inside the bandages and press his head forward. Then one more dreadful gnashing of his teeth and one more horrible groan and—the long ward was at length as silent as an empty church.

When the flaxen-haired assistant returned from the operating-room Miska's whining informed him from afar that another cot in the officers' division was now vacant. The im-

patient old Major quite needlessly beckoned
him to his side and announced in a loud voice
so that all the gentlemen could hear:

"The poor devil there has at last come to the
end of his sufferings." Then he added in a
voice vibrating with respect: "He died like a
true   Hungarian — singing   the   Rakoczy
March."

HOME AGAIN

VI

HOME AGAIN

A T last the lake gleamed through the leaves, and the familiar grey chalk mountains emerged into view, reaching out across the railroad embankment as with threatening fingers deep down into the water. There, beyond the smoky black opening of the short tunnel, the church steeple and a corner of the castle peeped for an instant above the grove.

John Bogdán leaned way out of the train window and looked at everything with greedy eyes, like a man going over the inventory of his possessions, all tense and distrustful, for fear something may have been lost in his absence. As each group of trees for which he waited darted by, he gave a satisfied nod, measuring the correctness of the landscape by the picture of it that he carried fairly seared in his

memory. Everything agreed. Every mile-
stone on the highroad, now running parallel
to the railroad tracks, stood ·on the right spot.
There! The flash of the flaming red copper
beech, at which the horses always shied and
once came within an ace of upsetting the carriage.

John Bogdán drew a deep, heavy sigh, fished
a small mirror out of his pocket, and gave his
face a final scrutiny before leaving the train.
At each station his face seemed to grow uglier.
The right side was not so bad. A bit of his
mustache still remained, and his right cheek
was fairly smooth except for the gash at the
corner of his mouth, which had not healed
properly. But the left side! He had let those
damned city folk tell him a whole lot of nonsense about the left side of his face. A bunch
of damned scoundrels they were, bent upon
making fools of poor peasants, in wartime just
the same as in peacetime—all of them, the
great doctor as well as the fine ladies in their
dazzling white gowns and with their silly af-

fected talk. Heaven knows it was no great
trick to bamboozle a simple coachman, who had
managed with only the greatest pains to learn a
bit of reading and writing. They had smiled
and simpered at him and were so nice and had
promised him such a paradise. And now, here
he was helpless, left all alone to himself, a lost
man.

With a furious curse, he tore off his hat and
threw it on the seat.

Was that the face of a human being? Was
it permitted to do such a thing to a man? His
nose looked like a patchwork of small dice of
different colors. His mouth was awry, and the
whole left cheek was like a piece of bloated raw
meat, red and criss-crossed with deep scars.
Ugh! How ugly! A fright! And besides, instead of a cheekbone, he had a long hollow,
deep enough to hold a man's finger. And it
was for this he had let himself be tortured so?
For this he had let himself be enticed seventeen times, like a patient sheep, into that confounded room with the glass walls and the shin-

ing instruments? A shudder ran down his
back at the recollection of the tortures he had
gone through with clenched teeth, just to look
like a human being again and be able to go
back home to his bride.

And now he *was* home.

The train pulled out of the tunnel, the whistle blew, and the dwarf acacias in front of the
station-master's hut sent a greeting through the
window. Grimly John Bogdán dragged his
heavy bag through the train corridor, descended the steps hesitatingly, and stood there
at a loss, looking around for help as the train
rolled on behind his back.

He took out his large flowered handkerchief
and wiped off the heavy beads of perspiration
from his forehead. What was he to do now?
Why had he come here at all? Now that he
had finally set foot again on the home soil for
which he had yearned so ardently, a great
longing came over him for the hospital, which
he had left that very morning, only a few hours
before, full of rejoicing. He thought of the

long ward with all those men wrapped in bandages who limped and hobbled, lame, blind or disfigured. There nobody was revolted by the sight of his mutilated face, no indeed. On the contrary, most of them envied him. He was at least capable of going back to work, his arms and legs were sound, and his right eye was perfect. Many would have been ready to exchange places with him. Some had begrudged him his lot and said it was wrong for the government to have granted him a pension on account of losing his left eye. One eye and a face a little scratched up—what was that compared with a wooden leg, a crippled arm, or a perforated lung, which wheezed and rattled like a poor machine at the slightest exertion?

Among the many cripples in the hospital John Bogdán was looked upon as a lucky devil, a celebrity. Everybody knew his story. The visitors to the hospital wanted first of all to see the man who had had himself operated on seventeen times and the skin cut away in

bands from his back, his chest, and his thighs.
After each operation, as soon as the bandages
were removed, the door to his ward never remained shut, a hundred opinions were pro-
nounced, and every newcomer was given a de-
tailed description of how terrible his face had
been before.   The few men who had shared
Bogdán's room with him from the start described the former awfulness of his face with
a sort of pride, as though they had taken part
in the successful operations.

Thus John Bogdán had gradually become
almost vain of his shocking mutilation and the
progress of the beautifying process. And when
he left the hospital, it was with the expectation
of being admired as a sensation in his village.

And now?

Alone in the world, with no relatives to go
to, with nothing but his knapsack and his little
trunk, the brilliant sunlight of the Hungarian
plain country flooding down on him, and the
village stretching away to a distance before
him, John Bogdán suddenly felt himself a prey

to timidity, to a terror that he had not known
amid the bursting of the shells, the most violent
charges, the most ferocious hand-to-hand encounters. His inert peasant intellect, his nature crudely compounded of wilfulness and
vanity, had always been a stranger to deep-
going reflections. Yet an instinctive misgiv-
ing, the sense of distrust and hostility that over-
whelmed him, told him plainly enough that he
was about to face disillusionment and mortifi-
cation such as he had not dreamed of in the
hospital.

He lifted his luggage to his back dejectedly
and walked toward the exit with hesitating
steps. There, in the shadow of the dusty acacias that he had seen grow up and that had
seen him grow up, he felt himself confronted
with his former self, with the handsome John
Bogdán who was known in the village as the
smart coachman of the manor. A lot of good
were all the operations and patchwork now.
The thing now was the painful contrast between the high-spirited, forward lad, who on

this spot had sung out a last hoarse farewell
to his sweetheart, Marcsa, on the first day of
mobilization, and the disfigured creature who
was standing in front of the same railroad station with one eye gone, a shattered cheekbone, a
patched-up cheek, and half a nose, embittered
and cast down, as if it were only that morning that he had met with the misfortune.

At the small grille gate stood the wife of the
station-guard, Kovacs—since the beginning of
the war Kovacs himself had been somewhere
on the Russian front—talking and holding the
ticket-puncher, impatiently waiting for the last
passenger to pass through. John Bogdán saw
her, and his heart began to beat so violently
that he involuntarily lingered at each step.
Would she recognize him, or would she not?
His knee joints gave way as if they had suddenly decayed, and his hand trembled as he
held out the ticket.

She took the ticket and let him pass through
—without a word!

Poor John Bogdán's breath stopped short.

But he pulled himself together with all his might, looked her firmly in the face with his one eye and said, with a painful effort to steady his voice:

"How do you do?"

"How do you do?" the woman rejoined. He encountered her eyes, saw them widen into a stare, saw them grope over his mangled face, and then quickly turn in another direction, as if she could not bear the sight. He wanted to stop, but he noticed her lips quiver and heard a murmured "Jesus, son of Mary," as if he were the devil incarnate. And he tottered on, deeply wounded.

"She did not recognize me!" the blood hammered in his ears. "She did not recognize me —did not recognize me!" He dragged himself to the bench opposite the station, threw his luggage to the ground and sank down on the seat.

She did not recognize him! The wife of Kovacs, the station-guard, did not recognize John Bogdán. The house of her parents stood next to the house of his parents. She and he had gone to school together, they had been confirmed together. He had held her in his arms and kissed and kissed her, heaven knows how many times, before Kovacs came to the village to woo her. And *she* had not recognized him! Not even by his voice, so great was the change.

He glanced over at her again involuntarily, and saw her talking eagerly with the station-master. From her gestures, he guessed she was telling of the horrible sight she had just seen, the stranger soldier so hideously disfigured. He uttered a short croaking sound, an abortive curse, and then his head fell on his chest, and he sobbed like a deserted woman.

What was he to do? Go up to the castle, open the door to the servants' quarters, and call out a saucy "Hello, Marcsa" to the astonished girl?

That was the way he had always thought of it. The devil knows how often he had painted the picture to the dot—the maids' screaming, Marcsa's cry of delight, her flinging her arms about his neck, and the thousand questions that would come pouring down on him, while he would sit there with Marcsa on his knees, and now and then throw out a casual reply to his awed, attentive listeners.

But now—how about it now? Go to Marcsa? He? 'With that face, the face that had made Julia, the station-guard's wife, cross herself in fright? Wasn't Marcsa famed throughout the county for her sharp tongue and haughty ways? She had snubbed the men by the score, laughed at them, made fools of them all, until she finally fell in love with him.

John Bogdán thrust his fist into his mouth and dug his teeth into the flesh, until the pain of it at length helped him subdue his sobbing. Then he buried his head in his hands and tried to think.

Never in his life had anything gone amiss with him. He had always been liked, at school, in the castle, and even in the barracks. He had gone through life whistling contentedly, a good-looking alert lad, an excellent jockey, and a coachman who drove with style and loved his horses, as his horses loved him. When he deigned to toss a kiss to the women as he dashed by, he was accustomed to see a flattered smile come to their faces. Only with Marcsa did it take a little longer. But she was famous for her beauty far and wide. Even John's master, the lord of the castle, had patted him on the shoulder almost enviously when Marcsa and he had become engaged.

"A handsome couple," the pastor had said.

John Bogdán groped again for the little mirror in his pocket and then sat with drooping body, oppressed by a profound melancholy. That thing in the glass was to be the bridegroom of the beautiful Marcsa? What did that ape's face, that piece of patchwork, that checkerboard which the damned quack, the impostor, whom they called a distinguished medical authority, a celebrated doctor, had basted together—what did it have to do with *that* John Bogdán whom Marcsa had promised to marry and whom she had accompanied to the station crying when he had gone off to the war? For Marcsa there was only *one* John Bogdán, the one that was coachman to the lord of the castle and the handsomest man in the village. Was he still coachman? The lord would take care not to disgrace his magnificent pair with such a scarecrow or drive to the county seat with such a monstrosity on the box. Haying—that's what they would put him to—cleaning out the dung from the stables. And Marcsa, the beautiful Marcsa whom all the men were vying for, would she be the wife of a miserable day laborer?

No, of this John Bogdán was certain, the man sitting on the bench there was no longer John Bogdán to Marcsa. She would not have him now—no more than the lord would have him on the coachman's box. A cripple is a cripple, and Marcsa had engaged herself to John Bogdán, not to the fright that he was bringing back home to her.

His melancholy gradually gave way to an ungovernable fury against those people in the city who had given him all that buncombe and talked him into heaven knows what. Marcsa should be proud because he had been disfigured in the service of his fatherland. Proud? Ha-ha!

He laughed scornfully, and his fingers tightened convulsively about the cursed mirror, until the glass broke into bits and cut his hand. The blood trickled slowly down his sleeves without his noticing it, so great was his rage against that bunch of aristocratic ladies in the hospital whose twaddle had deprived him of his reason. They probably thought that a man with one eye and half a nose was good enough for a peasant girl? Fatherland? Would Marcsa go to the altar with the fatherland? Could she show off the fatherland to the women when she would see them looking at her pityingly? Did the fatherland drive through the village with ribbons flying from its hat? Ridiculous!

Sitting on the bench opposite the station, with the sign of the village in view, a short

name, a single word, which comprised his whole
life, all his memories, hopes and experiences,
John Bogdán suddenly thought of one of the
village characters, Peter the cripple, who had
lived in the tumbledown hut behind the mill
many years before, when John was still a child.
John saw him quite distinctly, standing there
with his noisy wooden leg and his sad, starved,
emaciated face.   He, too, had sacrificed a part
of himself, his leg, "for the fatherland," in
Bosnia during the occupation; and then he had
had to live in the old hovel all alone, made fun
of by the children, who imitated his walk, and
grumblingly tolerated by the peasants, who
resented the imposition of this burden upon the
community.   "In the service of the fatherland."   Never had the "fatherland" been men-
tioned when Peter the cripple went by.   They
called him contemptuously the village pauper,
and that was all there was to it.

John Bogdán gnashed his teeth in a rage
that he had not thought of Peter the cripple
in the hospital.   Then he would have given

those city people a piece of his mind. He would have told them what he thought of their silly, prattling humbug about the fatherland and about the great honor it was to return home to Marcsa looking like a monkey. If he had the doctor in his clutches now! The fakir had photographed him, not once, but a dozen times, from all sides, after each butchery, as though he had accomplished a miracle, had turned out a wonderful masterpiece. And here Julia, even Julia, his playmate, his neighbor, had not recognized him.

So deep was John Bogdán sunk in his misery, so engulfed in grim plans of vengeance, that he did not notice a man who had been standing in front of him for several minutes, eyeing him curiously from every angle. Suddenly a voice woke him up out of his brooding, and a hot wave surged into his face, and his heart stood still with delighted terror, as he heard some one say:

"Is that you, Bogdán?"

He raised himself, happy at having been rec-

ognized after all. But the next moment he
knitted his brows in complete disappointment.
It was Mihály the humpback.

There was no other man in the whole village, even in the whole county, whose hand
John Bogdán would not at that moment have
grasped cordially in a surge of gratitude. But
this humpback—he never had wanted to have
anything to do with him, and now certainly
not. The fellow might imagine he had found
a comrade, and was probably glad that he was
no longer the only disfigured person in the
place.

"Yes, it's I. Well?"

The humpback's small, piercing eyes
searched Bogdán's scarred face curiously, and
he shook his head in pity.

"Well, well, the Russians certainly have done
you up."

Bogdán snarled at him like a vicious cur.

"It's none of your business. What right
have you to talk? If I had come into the
world like you, with my belly on my back, the

Russians couldn't have done anything to me."

The humpback seated himself quietly beside John without showing the least sign of being insulted.

"The war hasn't made you any politer, I can see that," he remarked drily. "You're not exactly in a happy frame of mind, which does not surprise me. Yes, that's the way it is. The poor people must give up their sound flesh and bone so that the enemy should not deprive the rich of their superfluity. You may bless your stars you came out of it as well as you did."

"I do," Bogdán growled with a glance of hatred. "The shells don't ask if you are rich or poor. Counts and barons are lying out there, rotting in the sun like dead beasts. Any man that God has not smitten in his cradle so that he's not fit to be either a man or a woman is out in the battlefield now, whether he's as poor as a church mouse or used to eating from golden plates."

The humpback cleared his throat and shrugged his shoulders.

"There are all sorts of people," he observed, and was about to add something else, but bethought himself and remained silent.

This Bogdán always had had the soul of a flunkey, proud of being allowed to serve the high and mighty and feeling solid with his oppressors because he was allowed to contribute to their pomp in gold-laced livery and silver buttons. His masters had sicked him on to face the cannons in defense of their own wealth, and now the man sat there disfigured, with only one eye, and still would not permit any criticism of his gracious employers. Against such stupidity there was nothing to be done. There was no use wasting a single word on him.

The two remained sitting for a while in silence. Bogdán filled his pipe carefully and deliberately, and Mihály watched him with interest.

"Are you going to the castle?" the humpback asked cautiously, when the pipe was at last lit.

John Bogdán was well aware just what the hateful creature was aiming at. He knew him. A Socialist—that's what he was, one of those good-for-nothings who take the bread out of poor people's mouths by dinning a lot of nonsense into their ears, just like a mean dog who snaps at the hand that feeds him. He had made a good living as foreman in the brickyard, and as thanks he had incited all the workmen against the owner, Bogdán's master, until they demanded twice as much wages, and were ready to set fire to the castle on all four corners. Once Mihály had tried his luck with him, too. He had wanted to make his master out a bad man. But this time he had bucked up against the right person. A box on his right ear and a box on his left ear, and then a good sound kick—that was the answer to keep him from ever again trying to make a Socialist of John Bogdán, one of those low fellows who know no God or fatherland.

Mihály moved on the bench uneasily, every now and then scrutinizing his neighbor from the side. At last he plucked up courage and said suddenly:

"They'll probably be glad up there that you are back. Your arms are still whole, and they need people in the factory."

Bogdán turned up his nose.

"In the brickyard?" he asked disdainfully.

The humpback burst out laughing.

"Brickyard? Brickyard is good. Who needs bricks in war? The brickyard's gone long ago, man. Do you see those trucks over there? They are all loaded up with shells. Every Saturday a whole train of shells leaves here."

Bogdán listened eagerly. That was news. A change on the estate of which he had not yet heard.

"You see, there is such a nice division," Mihály continued, smiling sarcastically. "One goes away and lets his head be blown off. The other remains comfortably at home and manufactures shells and decorates his castle with thousand-dollar bills. Well, I'm satisfied."

"What are we to do, eh, shoot with peas or with air? You can't carry on a war without shells. Shells are needed just as much as soldiers."

"Exactly. And because the rich have the choice of being soldiers or making shells, they choose to make the shells and send *you* off to have your head blown off. What are you getting for your eye? Twenty-five dollars a year? Or perhaps as much as fifty? And the others whom the ravens are feeding on don't get even that out of the war. But the gentleman up in the castle is making his five hundred a day and doesn't risk even his little finger doing it. I'd be a patriot on those terms myself. I am telling you the truth. At first, of course, they said he was going to war, and he did actually ride off in great state, but three weeks later he was back here again with machines and all the equipment, and now he delivers fine orations in the townhouse and sends

other men off to die—and on top of it is gallant
to the wives left behind. He stuffs his pockets
and fools with every girl in the factory. He's
the cock of the whole district."

Bogdán, his brows knit in annoyance, let the
man talk on. But the last part struck him
with a shock. He pricked up his ears and
grew uneasy and for a while struggled heroi-
cally against asking a question that burned on
his lips. But in the end he could not restrain
himself and blurted out:

"Is—is Marcsa working in the factory,
too?"

The humpback's eyes flashed.

"Marcsa, the beautiful Marcsa! I should
say so! She's been made a forelady, though
they say she's never had a shell in her hands,
but, to make up, the lord's hands have——"

With a short, hoarse growl John Bogdán
flew at the humpback's throat, squeezed in his
Adam's apple, pressing it into his neck, and
held him in a merciless clutch. The man beat
about with his arms, his eyes popped from his

head in fright, his throat gurgled, and his face turned livid. Then John Bogdán released his hold, and Mihály fell to the ground and lay there gasping. Bogdán quickly gathered up his things and strode off, taking long, quick steps, as if afraid of arriving too late for something in the castle.

He gave not another look back at Mihály the humpback, never turned around once, but quietly went his way and for a long while felt the warm throat in his hand.

What was a man who lay gasping on the road to him? One man more or less. In the rhythmic regularity of the marching column, he had passed by thousands like him, and it had never occurred to his mind, dulled by weariness, that the grey spots thickly strewn over the fields, the heaps lining the roadway like piles of dung in the spring, were human beings struck down by death. He and his comrades had waded in the dead, there at Kielce, when they made a dash across the fields, and earthy grey hands rose out of every furrow pawing the air, and trousers drenched in blood and distorted faces grew out of the ground, as if all the dead were scrambling from their graves for the Last Judgment. They had stepped and stumbled over corpses. Once the fat little officer of reserves, to the great amusement of his company, had gotten deathly sick at his stomach because he had inadvertently stepped on the chest of a half-decayed Russian, and the body had given way under him, and he had scarcely been able to withdraw his foot from the foul hole. John Bogdán smiled as he recalled the wicked jokes the men had cracked at the officer's expense, how the officer had gone all white and leaned against a tree and carried on like a man who has much more than quenched his thirst.

The road glowed in the mid-day sun. The village clock struck twelve. From the hill yonder came, like an answer, the deep bellow of the factory whistle, and a little white cloud rose over the tops of the trees. Bogdán quickened his pace, running rather than walking, heedless of the drops of sweat that ran down and tickled his neck.   For almost a year he had breathed nothing but the hospital atmosphere, had smelled nothing but iodoform and lysol and seen nothing but roofs and walls.   His lungs drew in the aroma of the blossoming meadows with deep satisfaction, and the soles of his boots tramped the ground sturdily, as if he were again marching in regular order.

This was the first walk he had taken since he was wounded, the first road he had seen since those wild marches on Russian soil.   At moments he seemed to hear the cannons roaring.   The short struggle with the humpback had set his blood coursing, and his memories of the war, for a time stifled as it were beneath a layer of dust by the dreary monotony of the hospital life, suddenly came whirling back to him.

He almost regretted having let that damned blackguard go so soon.   One moment more, and he would never have opened his blasphemous mouth again.   His head would have fallen back exhausted to one side, he would once again have embraced the air longingly with outspread fingers, and then in a flash would have shrunk together, exactly like the fat, messy Russian with the large blue eyes who was the first man to present himself to St. Peter with a greeting from John Bogdán. Bogdán had not let *him* loose until he had altogether quit squirming. He had choked him dead as a doornail. And still he was a comical fellow, not nearly so disgusting as that rascally humpback. But he was the first enemy soldier whom he had got into his grasp, his very first Russian. A magnificent array of others had followed, though the fat man was the only one Bogdán had choked to death. He had smashed scores with the butt-end of his gun and run his bayonet through scores of others. He had even squashed with his boots the wretch who had struck down his dearest comrade before his very eyes. But never again did he choke a man to death. That was why the little fat fellow stuck in his memory. He had no recol-

lection of the others whatever. All he saw now
in his mind was a tangle of greyish-green uniforms. And as he thought of his heroic deeds,
the gnashing, the stamping, the gasping, and
the cursing of the hand-to-hand encounters resounded in his ears. How many, he wondered,
had he sent to the other world? God alone
may have counted them. He himself had had
enough to do trying to save his own skin.
Had a man stopped to look around, he would
have carried his curiosity to the next world.

And yet—there was another face that remained fixed in his memory. A great big thin
fellow, as tall as a beanpole, with enormous
yellow tusks, which he gnashed like a boar.
Yes, he had as clear a picture of him as if
it had been yesterday. He saw him half-
backed up against the wall already, swinging
his gun over his head. One second more, and
the butt-end would have come whizzing down.
But a sleepy Russian was never the man to
get the better of John Bogdán. Before he
had the chance to bring down his gun, Bog-

dán's bayonet was in between his ribs, and the
Russian fell over on his own gun. The bayonet pierced him through and through, and
even went into the wall behind him, and came
mighty near breaking off.

But the same thing never happened to Bogdán again. It had happened that once because he had thrust too hard, with clenched
teeth, gripping the rod in a tight clutch, as if it
were iron that he had to cleave. The fact was,
he had not yet discovered that it really isn't so
difficult to mow down a human being. He had
been prepared for any amount of resistance,
and his bayonet had glided into the fellow's
body like butter. His mouth had remained
wide open in astonishment—he recalled it to
the dot. A man who has never tried a bayonet
thrust thinks a human being is made up all
of bones, and he fetches out for a good hard
stroke. Then he's in a pickle to free his
weapon again before one of the messy-looking
devils takes advantage of his defenselessness.
The way to do was to go at it very lightly, with

a short jerky thrust. Then the blade ran in
of itself, like a good horse—you actually had
trouble holding it back. The most important
thing was, not to take your eye off your
enemy. You mustn't look at your bayonet, or
the spot you intend to pierce. You must always watch your enemy so as to guess his move
in time. It's from your enemy's face that you
must read the right moment for stepping backward. They all behaved the same way—exactly like the first tall wild fellow who gnashed
his tusks. All of a sudden their faces turned
absolutely smooth, as if the cold iron in their
body had chilled their fury, their eyes opened
wide in astonishment and looked at their enemy
as if to ask in reproach, "What are you doing?" Then they usually clutched at the bayonet and needlessly cut their fingers, too, before they fell over dead. If you didn't know
exactly what to do and didn't hold your weapon
back in time and withdraw it quickly from the
wound, just when you saw the man's eyes
growing large, you would be carried along

down with him or would get hit on the head by the butt-end of another enemy's gun long before you could draw your bayonet out.

These were all things that John Bogdán had often discussed with his comrades after severe frays when they criticized the men who had fallen for behaving stupidly and who had had to pay with their lives for their awkwardness.

As he strode along in haste up the familiar road to the castle, he was fairly lost in recollections. His legs moved of themselves, like horses on the homeward way. He passed through the open grille gateway and was already walking on the gravel path, his head bowed on his chest, without noticing that he had reached home.

The neighing of horses woke him up from his thoughts with a start. He stood still, deeply stirred by the sight of the stables, only a few feet away, and inside, in the twilight, the gleam of his favorite horse's flanks. He was about to turn off the path and make for the stable door when far away down below, at the

other end of the large place, he saw a woman
coming from the brickyard. She wore a dotted
red silk kerchief on her head and carried her
full figure proudly, and the challenging sway
of her hips billowed her wide skirts as the wind
billows a field of ripe grain.

John Bogdán stood stockstill, as if some one
had struck him on the chest. It was Marcsa!
There was not another girl in the whole country who walked like that. He threw his luggage to the ground and dashed off.

"Marcsa! Marcsa!" his cry thundered out
over the broad courtyard.

The girl turned and waited for his approach,
peering curiously through half-closed eyes.
When almost face to face with her Bogdán
stood still.

"Marcsa!" he repeated in a whisper, his gaze
fastened upon her face anxiously. He saw her
turn pale, white as chalk, saw her eyes leap to
and fro uneasily, from his left cheek to his right
cheek, and back again. Then horror came into
her eyes. She clapped her hands to her face,

and turned and ran away as fast as her legs
would carry her.

In utter sadness Bogdán stared after her.
That was exactly the way he had imagined their
meeting again since Julia, the station-guard's
wife, the woman he had grown up with, had
not recognized him.   But to run away!   That
rankled.   No need for her to run away.   John
Bogdán was not the man to force himself on a
woman.   If he no longer pleased her now that
he was disfigured, well, then she could look for
another man, and he, too—he would find another woman.   He wasn't bothered about that.

This was what he had wanted to tell Marcsa.

He bounded after her and overtook her a few
feet from the machine shop.

"Why do you run away from me?" he
growled, breathless, and caught her hand.
"If you don't want me any more, you need
only say so.   What do you think—I'm going
to eat you up?"

She stared at him searchingly—in uncertainty. He almost felt sorry for her, she was trembling so.

"How you look!" he heard her stammer, and he turned red with anger.

"You knew it. I had them write to you that a shell hit me. Did you think it made me better-looking? Just speak straight out if you don't want me any more. Straight wine is what I want, no mixture. Yes or no? I won't force you to marry me. Just say it right away—yes or no?"

Marcsa was silent. There was something in his face, in his one eye, that took her breath away, that dug into her vitals like cold fingers. She cast her eyes down and stammered:

"But you have no position yet. How can we marry? You must first ask the master if he——"

It was as if a red pall woven of flames dropped in front of John Bogdán's eyes. The master? What was she saying about the master? He thought of the humpback, and it came to him in a flash that the fellow had not

lied. His fingers clutched her wrist like a pair
of glowing tongs, so that she cried out with
the pain.

"The master!" Bogdán bellowed. "What
has the master got to do between you and me?
Yes or no? I want an answer. The master
has nothing to do with us."

Marcsa drew herself up. All of a sudden
a remarkable assurance came to her. The
color returned to her cheeks, and her eyes
flashed proudly. She stood there with the
haughty bearing so familiar to Bogdán, her
head held high in defiance.

Bogdán observed the change and saw that
her gaze traveled over his shoulder. He let
go her hand and turned instantly. Just what
he thought—the master coming out of the
machine shop. His old forester, Tóth, followed him.

Marcsa bounded past Bogdán like a cat and
ran up to the lord and bent over and kissed his
hand.

Bogdán saw the three of them draw near and

lowered his head like a ram for attack. A cold, determined quiet rose in him slowly, as in the trenches when the trumpeter gave the signal for a charge. He felt the lord's hand touch his shoulder, and he took a step backward.

What was the meaning of it all? The lord was speaking of heroism and fatherland, a lot of rubbish that had nothing to do with Marcsa. He let him go on talking, let the words pour down on him like rain, without paying any attention to their meaning. His glance wandered to and fro uneasily, from the lord to Marcsa and then to the forester, until it rested curiously on something shining.

It was the nickeled hilt of the hunting-knife hanging at the old forester's side and sparkling in the sunlight.

"Like a bayonet," thought Bogdán, and an idea flashed through his mind, to whip the thing out of the scabbard and run it up to the hilt in the hussy's body. But her rounded hips, her bright billowing skirts confused him. In war he had never had to do with women. He could not exactly imagine what it would be like to make a thrust into that beskirted body there. His glance traveled back to the master, and now he noticed that his stiffnecked silence had pulled him up short.

"He is gnashing his teeth," it struck him, "just like the tall Russian." And he almost smiled at a vision that came to his mind—of the lord also getting a smooth face and astonished, reproachful eyes.

But hadn't he said something about Marcsa just then? .What was Marcsa to him?

Bogdán drew himself up defiantly.

"I will arrange matters with Marcsa myself, sir. It's between her and me," he rejoined hoarsely, and looked his master straight in the face. *He* still had his mustache, quite even on the two sides, and curling delicately upwards at the ends. What was it the humpback had said? "One man goes away and lets his head be blown off." He wasn't so stupid after all, the humpback wasn't.

What Bogdán said infuriated the master.

Bogdán let him shout and stared like a man hypnotized at the nickeled hilt of the hunting-knife. It was not until the name "Marcsa" again struck his ear that he became attentive.

"Marcsa is in my employ now," he heard the lord saying. "You know I am fond of you, Bogdán. I'll let you take care of the horses again, if you care to. But Marcsa is to be let alone. I won't have any rumpus. If she still wants to marry you, all well and good. But if she doesn't, she's to be let alone. If I hear once again that you have annoyed her, I'll chase you to the devil. Do you understand?"

Foaming with rage, Bogdán let out the stream of his wrath.

"To the devil?" he shouted. "You chase me to the devil? You had first better go there yourself. I've been to the devil already. For eight months I was in hell. Here's my face— you can tell from my face that I come from hell. To play the protector here and stuff your pockets full and send the others out to die—that's easy. A man who dawdles at home has no right to send men to the devil who have already been in hell for his sake."

So overwhelming was his indignation that he spoke like the humpback Socialist and was not ashamed of it. He stood there ready to leap, with tensely drawn muscles, like a wild animal. He saw the lord make ready to strike him, saw his distorted face, saw the riding-crop flash through the air, and even saw it descending upon him. But he did not feel the short, hard blow on his back.

With one bound he ripped the hunting-knife out of the scabbard and thrust it between the lord's ribs—not with a long sweep, so that some one could have stayed his arm before he struck. Oh, no! But quite lightly, from below, with a short jerk, exactly as he had learned by experience in battle. The hunting-knife was as good as his bayonet. It ran into the flesh like butter.

Then everything came about just as it always did. John Bogdán stood with his chin forward and saw the lord's face distorted by

anger suddenly smooth out and turn as placid
and even as if it had been ironed. He saw his
eyes widen and look over at him in astonishment with the reproachful question, "What
are you doing?" The one thing Bogdán did
not see was the collapsing of the lord's body,
for at that instant a blow crashed down on the
back of his head, like the downpour of a waterfall dropping from an infinite height. For one
second he still saw Marcsa's face framed in a
fiery wheel, then, his skull split open, he fell
over on top of his master, whose body already
lay quivering on the ground.